Pompeii
The Day a City Died

Pompeii

It was the 24th day of August in the year A.D. 79. It was hot, unnaturally hot, for a summer's dawn. A violent tremor shook the burning air, followed by a clap of thunder. The people of Pompeii, Italy, watched, horrified, as Mount Vesuvius burst open before their very eyes. White-hot stones hailed down upon the town. Then came the ash, blinding them, choking their mouths and lungs. Some took cover in the farthest corners of their homes; others tried to escape, fleeing toward the nearby sea. But very few would get that far.

Near the Nucerian Gate one family, like many others, was desperately attempting to leave the city. Their slave, walking beside them, made a vain attempt to protect himself from the burning cinders with a fallen roof tile. Inexorably, the ash continued to pile up, mounting to the level of house windows, blocking doorways. Before long, it had buried even the rooftops. Terror was extinguished in death; men, women, children, and animals, frozen in their final agony, were transformed into inanimate matter.

cbroulin.

Pompeii, 1961

Almost two thousand years passed before the archaeologist Amedeo Maiuri found this family. The slave still held the tile that had failed to protect him; the women and children lay hand in hand. One man, who had clearly fought to the very end, was still propping himself up on his elbow in a final effort to rise and help his loved ones.

CONTENTS

POMPEII
THE DAY A CITY DIED

Robert Etienne

DISCOVERIES

HARRY N. ABRAMS, INC., PUBLISHERS

NEW YORK

Very soon after 24 August 79, judging by the available evidence, Pompeii disappeared completely from the face of the inhabited world. On the leveled earth, grass and vines gradually took possession of land where the town had once stood. Country people soon forgot even its name, referring to the hill that now covered it by the blanket term *la città*, "the city."

CHAPTER I
THE HUNT FOR TREASURES

The death of the city meant not only the destruction of its streets, monuments, and houses, but also the death of its inhabitants, struck down in the midst of their everyday activities; their contorted forms were faithfully preserved by the volcanic ash spewed out by Vesuvius.

Chronicle of a Famous Death: Pliny the Elder

"They decided to go down to the shore, to see at first hand whether it was possible to escape by sea; but they found the waves still wild and dangerous. There a sheet was spread on the ground for my uncle to lie down on, and he called repeatedly for cold water, which he drank. Then the flames and smell of sulfur which heralded the approaching fire drove the others to take flight. Aroused, my uncle struggled to his feet, leaning on two slaves, but immediately collapsed. I assume that his breathing was impeded by the dense fumes, which choked his windpipe— for it was constitutionally weak and narrow, and often inflamed. When daylight returned—two days after the last time he had seen it—his body was found intact and uninjured, still fully clothed as in life. He looked more like a man who is sleeping than a dead man."

Pliny the Younger
Letter to Tacitus
A.D. 104

Romantic Visions Inspired by the Ruins

If the people who escaped from Pompeii had returned to the scene of the disaster, they would have found no trace of their city, which lay buried beneath the dense layer of ash that had accumulated between 10 A.M. and 1 P.M. on 24 August 79. Yet 19th-century painters often chose to evoke the memory of the dead city by combining—as in this painting by Paul Alfred de Curzon, *Dream Amid the Ruins of Pompeii*—a typically romanticized vision of the ruins with figures in ancient dress, bewailing the tragic fate of their familiar haunts.

Graffiti reveal that even in the immediate aftermath of the eruption, teams went in to try to recover the most valuable objects from Pompeii, but only in the 18th century was Europe seized with a virtual passion to reveal the lost cities of Pompeii and Herculaneum.

Sack and Pillage of a Buried City—With the Kings' Permission

The ruins of Herculaneum had first been discovered in 1594, but it was not until 1709 that serious excavations began. At that time southern Italy was dominated by Austria, and it was the Austrian rulers of Naples who had shafts and tunnels dug in order to plunder statues; they then exported the statues to their Viennese residences. They cared little if, in the process, great holes were smashed in walls covered with paintings. Only one brave voice was raised against this pillage: that of the pope.

Unfortunately, the treasure hunting was renewed when Charles III of Spain, king of the Two Sicilies, sent Rocco Gioacchino de Alcubierre, a surveying engineer, to supply the Spanish court with statues and precious objects. In 1748 the first site was opened in Pompeii roughly 650 feet from the Temple of Fortuna Augusta, close to the Via Stabiana and the Via di Nola (see map on pp. 46–7). This was soon abandoned, however, as Alcubierre decided to transfer his attention to Herculaneum, and it was not until 1754 that excavations at Pompeii were renewed. Only nine years later, thanks to the discovery of an inscription, did *la città* regain its true name of Pompeii.

The Intelligentsia Flocked to Pompeii and Herculaneum—Not Always for the Right Reasons

By this time, Europe, alerted by the early visitors to Pompeii, was hungry for details. Scholars began to make the journey to Naples, and the city soon became an important stop on the Grand Tour, which was fashionable for aristocrats to make. The excavations nearby were later to play an important part in the Neoclassical revival, as artists, architects, furniture makers, and potters, such as Wedgwood, drew

The village of Resina was built on top of the solidified torrent of mud that put an abrupt end to all life in Herculaneum. Alcubierre's team of "excavators" (above) fought their way through this wall of mud, which was as hard as petrified lava and 26 feet thick, cutting into it to create staircases and ramps, trenches and underground passages.

The mysterious buried city regained its true name thanks to the discovery of an inscription. The Italian artist Giovanni Battista Piranesi immediately introduced the name into one of his engravings.

inspiration from Pompeii. Some of Robert Adam's interiors, for example, were based on the frescoed walls and stucco work of Pompeii.

Yet the excavations were far from exemplary; Johann Joachim Winckelmann, the great German archaeologist, made no bones about protesting at the anarchy that ruled there (see p. 146). It was Karl Weber, director of the excavations at Pompeii, who first proposed that, rather than carrying out selective and uncoordinated digs, they should uncover the site systematically, section by section. In this way a tavern, the Tomb of the Istacidii, and that of the priestess Mamia were discovered close to the Herculaneum Gate. The imagination of Europe was set ablaze by these discoveries. Weber's successor, the Spaniard Francesco La Vega, discovered the Odeon, or small theater, in 1764, and then the Temple of Isis, reconstructed after the earthquake of 62 by Popidius Celsinus; in 1767 the gladiators' barracks were uncovered. La Vega established the first overall plan of the excavations—indicating an increasingly rational approach to the work—and in spite of the limited workforce at his disposal, the Odeon and the large theater had been completely cleared by 1789. Yet still the aim was to find precious objects, and once the purpose of a particular building had been established, its excavation was abandoned.

Between 1770 and 1815 the excavations were given new impetus under the influence of the Neapolitan

The road from Pompeii to Herculaneum was the first to be uncovered; beside it was discovered a group of tombs, the necropolis outside the Herculaneum Gate. The mausoleum in the process of being disinterred and restored here (left) is that of the Istacidii; it stands on a low terrace surrounded by a stone balustrade. The vast burial chamber is decorated externally with fluted engaged columns. The solidity of the structure gives some impression of the wealth of this family, which was connected with some of the most important names in Pompeian society.

The Temple of Isis (above right) was discovered in 1765, together with an inscription naming the person responsible for its reconstruction after the earthquake of 5 February 62. This watercolor was painted by Sir William Hamilton, English ambassador to the court of Naples, whose life as a diplomat clearly left him sufficient time to visit the excavations.

kings and their wives. Caroline, daughter of Maria Theresa of Austria and wife of the weak and ineffectual Ferdinand I of the Two Sicilies, showed keen interest in the excavations. The Villa of Diomedes was uncovered in 1771, and in 1772 eighteen bodies were discovered in an underground passage; among them was that of a young girl, who inspired the French romantic novelist Théophile Gautier to write the novella *Arria Marcella* in 1852.

The fame of Pompeii spread: Goethe visited it in 1787, while Sir William Hamilton, English ambassador to the court of Naples from 1764 to 1800, was a regular and enthusiastic observer at the site.

The writings of Johann Joachim Winckelmann (left, 1717–68), author of a *History of Ancient Art*, helped to spread throughout Europe a taste for the classical world. His critical comments made him unpopular with the Neapolitan court, however. He claimed that Alcubierre knew as much about antiquity as "the moon knows about lobsters," and, referring to the speed at which work on the excavations was progressing, he wrote: "At this rate our great-grandchildren will still have plenty of work to do." Nevertheless, thanks to Hamilton, he was allowed to watch the excavation of what would later be recognized as the gladiators' barracks.

Like many painters of his generation, Jacob Philipp Hackert (1737–1807) visited Italy early on as part of his Grand Tour. In this painting, which shows the theater quarter of Pompeii, he reveals the stage excavations had reached by 1799. Thanks to the efforts of the Spaniard La Vega, excavation of the Odeon, or covered theater (the rectangular building on the left), and of the large theater (on the right), first discovered in 1764, was finally completed in 1789. The semicircular corridor that gave access to the upper levels of the large theater is clearly visible. The central courtyard of the gladiators' barracks (behind the Odeon) is surrounded by a colonnade, and on the far right, in the foreground, stand the remains of the Temple of Isis. On the horizon can be seen the Lattari mountains, where the rich Pompeian landowners grazed their flocks.

In Under a Decade Important Buildings Were Feverishly Brought to Light

In 1808 Joachim Murat and Queen Caroline, sister of Napoleon I, became rulers of Naples. Passionately interested in archaeology, they delved deep into their own pockets to speed up the excavations. The limits of the city were established; the outer wall was

Pompeii aroused everyone's curiosity. Grisly scenes were staged for early groups of tourists (above), who could also enjoy romantic walks around the Tomb of the Istacidii (above right).

excavated near the Via Consolare, and work continued on the amphitheater and the basilica. The Napoleonic royal family proved as fascinated by Pompeii as the early Bourbon rulers of Naples had been. But with the return of the old dynasty, work on the excavations slackened.

"The strangest thing I saw on my travels was Pompeii, where you feel as if you have been transported back into the ancient world; even if you normally believe only proven facts, here you feel as if, just by being there, you know more about the place than any scholar. What a great pleasure it is to come face to face with antiquity, when one has read so many books about it."

Stendhal
Rome, Naples, and Florence, 1817

La Vega died in 1815 and was replaced by Antonio Bonnucci, who in 1818 was working with only thirteen assistants. Yet Pompeii continued to attract the crowned heads of Europe, who were treated to fictitious on-the-spot "discoveries" of rooms that had been reburied only a few moments before their visit.

In 1823 the forum was excavated, together with the theater quarter, the remaining portion of the gladiators' barracks, the western wall, the area around the Herculaneum Gate, much of the Street of Tombs, the amphitheater, and the houses at the northern end of the Via Stabiana. In 1824 it was the turn of the Temple of Fortuna Augusta and the Forum Baths.

Francis I, king of the Two Sicilies from 1825 to 1830, showed more interest in Pompeii than his brother Ferdinand I had; a house to the north of the Forum Baths, a bakery, and the House of the Tragic Poet were uncovered during his reign. Under his successor, Ferdinand II, a vast mosaic depicting Alexander the Great at the Battle of Issus was found in the House of the Faun.

When Garibaldi entered Naples in 1861, overturning

To the west of the city stands the Herculaneum Gate (visible on the left of the plan opposite). The road to Herculaneum was made up of three lanes— two of which were reserved for pedestrians —and, for the first 650 feet outside the city, was bordered by tombs and shops. On the far right is the imposing Villa of Diomedes, the layout of which was reconstructed from details given in an early tax register. The rooms of this suburban villa were arranged around two peristyles. With its extensive garden, established on a lower level, it provided a foretaste of the country villas scattered over the slopes of Vesuvius.

LES RUINES
DE
POMPEI
DESSINÉES ET MESURÉES
PAR
F. MAZOIS

An Architect in Pompeii

François Mazois (1783–1826), author of *The Ruins of Pompeii*, trained as an architect under Claude-Nicolas Ledoux and Charles Percier. In 1808 he found himself in Naples, appointed by Murat to direct work on improvements to the city. It was here that he began to restore the ancient monuments of Campania. From 1809 to 1811 he devoted himself to Pompeii: "Here I am, settled in Pompeii once more, where, in spite of the heat, my riches continue to increase, that is, my collection of finds continues to grow.... I get up very early; at about 9 o'clock the fierce heat of the sun forces me to take a break, so I return to my small room, where I finish the sketches I have made during the morning. At midday my cook solemnly presents me with a vast plate of macaroni. After I have eaten that, an hour's sleep restores my good humor and enthusiasm, so I set to work again in my cramped lodgings until 5 o'clock, and then out in the windy open air until sunset. All in all, that means a total of thirteen or fourteen hours' work a day. So you can see I am working hard."

The Poetry of the Ruins

The 454 drawings Mazois made, which included views of monuments, plans, and studies of individual objects, were engraved and published between 1824 and 1838. The picture on p. 24 reveals the heart of a house in Pompeii, the atrium, whose roof would have been supported by the four columns visible in the center. The entrance can be seen on a line with the atrium; the stone bench in front of the house, on which a soldier is resting, is where visitors and clients would have waited to be received. In the house shown here an ornamental pool lies in the center of a garden surrounded by painted trompe-l'oeil pilasters.

"Just imagine: I was in Pompeii, perched on a narrow, ruined wall, when suddenly it shifted and then collapsed, throwing me straight down, head first, onto the antique marble floor beneath. I must confess, I can think of no better way to die, nor of any better place to be buried."

François Mazois
Letter to Mlle. Duval

the Bourbons, he offered the directorship of the museum and excavations to the French novelist Alexandre Dumas, author of *The Three Musketeers*. But Dumas was prepared to make only a short-term commitment to the post.

As Italy Is United Under Victor-Emmanuel II and Cavour, Pompeii's Fortunes Begin to Change

The new king of Italy was aware of the prestige that his dynasty would gain from well-organized excavations at Pompeii. On 20 December 1860 he put Giuseppe

Overall view of the excavations during the 19th century. In the foreground is the theater quarter, with the gladiators' barracks; in the center, a triumphal arch marks the position of the Temple of the Capitoline Triad and, therefore, the open square of the forum.

Fiorelli in charge of the excavations. Fiorelli was a young numismatist already known for his critical good sense and scientific integrity. He soon established a scientific approach to archaeology, keeping a written record of the excavations and preparing a careful plan for uncovering the

Just to the right of center in this print the S-curve of the Via Consolare contrasts with the regular gridlike layout of roads in the area just to the east of it.

In 1863 the excavations at Pompeii were the scene of intense activity. Hordes of workmen carry away the rubble in wicker baskets (left), while in the areas where buildings are being restored (right), builders are busy reconstructing roofs, righting columns, and relaying lintels.

It was around this time that Fiorelli invented a way of casting the bodies that had been buried in ash. Once the location of a body had been established, plaster was poured through a small hole until the cavity had been filled. It was thus discovered that the ash had, in solidifying around the bodies of both humans and animals, molded itself to their forms, defining every tiny fold of their clothes, every last twitch of their muscles.

Overleaf: The restoration of the Forum of Pompeii (cross-section). Detail of the Temple of Apollo.

site quarter by quarter and house by house, with the aid of over five hundred workmen. He divided Pompeii into regions and blocks, or *insulae*, allotting each house an identifying number; his system is still in use today.

To avoid the danger of houses collapsing into roads that had already been cleared, he excavated them from the roof downward, gradually removing all debris from the site. In 1863 he invented a method of plaster casting that preserved

General plan
1. Basilica
2. Temple of Apollo
3. Warehouse buildings
4. Latrines
5. City treasury
6. Commemorative arch
7. Temple of the Capitoline Triad
8. Arch of Tiberius
9. Macellum (market)
10. Sanctuary of the Lares
11. Temple of Vespasian
12. Building of Eumachia
13. Comitium
14. Office of the Aediles
15. Curia
16. Office of the Duoviri
17. Forum
18. Forum Baths
19. Temple of Fortuna Augusta
20. So-called Arch of Caligula
21. Via dell' Abbondanza
22. Shops

. ARC DE TIBERE .

MPLE DE JVPITER

RVM · COTE NORD ·

of the Capitoline Triad

L DE JVPITER

RVM · COTE NORD ·

2. Temple of Apollo

TEMPLE D'APOLLON

FORVM

COTE OUEST

8. Arch of Tiberius   9. *Macellum* (market)

RVE

MACELLVM

Longitudinal section from north to south
Through the Temple of the Capitoline Triad

1. Basilica

CVRIE

BASILIQVE

Elevation of the buildings
Viewed from the Via del Foro

22. Shops

20. So-called Arch of Caligula

19. Temple of Fortuna Augusta

RVE · TEMPLE DE LA FORTVNE ·

BOVTIQVES

RVE

The forum, which was brought to light from the early 19th century, was soon adopted in all the architectural academies of Europe as the very model of the classical square. This 1910 reconstruction was created by Léon Jaussely of Paris.

EDIFICE D'EVMACHIA · MARCHE · AVX · LAINES ·

12. Building of Eumachia

21. Via dell'Abbondanza

EDIFICE D'EVMACHIA

7. Temple of the Capitoline Triad

MARCHÉ

TEMPLE DE JVPITER

10. Sanctuary of the Lares   11. Temple of Vespasian   12. Building of

T·DES·DIEVX·LARES·PVBLICS   TEMPLE DE VESPASIEN   EDIFICE   D

FORVM   CÔTÉ EST

The Forum of Pompeii

Cross-section from east to west
Through the Temple of Apollo and the building of Eumachia: above, actual state (1910) and below, restoration

TEMPLE D'APOLLON

TE

FO

2. Temple of Apollo

7. Templ
17. Forur

TEMPL

FO

TEMPLE D'APOLLON

18. Forum Baths

BOVTIQVES   JARDIN   BAIN DES HOMMES   TEPIDARIVM   BOVTIQVES

THERMES DV FORVM

13. Comitium   16. Office of the Duoviri

A   COMITIVM   SALLE DES DVVMVIRS

the positions adopted by Pompeians in the moment of death. The most intimate details of daily life in the city could at last be revealed. Using these techniques, Fiorelli identified the Lupanar, or brothel, a bakery and the House of Caecilius Jucundus (V, 1). (This and all following references correspond to regions and *insulae* as indicated on the map on pp. 46–7.) In 1875 he took on overall control of the museums, leaving his students to complete his work, which had emphasized the topographical cohesion of the excavations.

A Pompeian Golden Age: 1875–93

Michele Ruggiero, an architect who had formerly worked with Fiorelli, sought to extend the excavations eastward toward the Nolan Gate by excavating the northernmost quarters of the city along the upper *decumanus*. In the process, the Central Baths were discovered. In Region IX the House of the Centenary (8)—so named to commemorate the 18th centenary of the eruption—and *insulae* 4, 5, 6, 7 and 8 were excavated, followed by those in Region V on the Via di Nola and the Via Stabiana (1, 2, 3, 4). The excavation of *insula* 2 in Region VIII proved extremely difficult, as in this area the houses, which were several stories high, were constructed on the slope of a hill formed by a prehistoric lava flow.

Another discovery of the 1880s were the cemeteries just outside the gates to the city; a few tombs were found near what is assumed to have been the road from Pompeii to Nocera (Nuceria), and two tombs were discovered at the Stabian Gate. Ruggiero was also responsible for the consolidation and restoration, in situ, of over six hundred paintings and of the atrium of the House of the Silver Wedding (V, 2) and the House of the Balcony (VII, 12).

A New Man in Charge: Epigraphist Giulio de Petra

De Petra directed work on the site from 1893 to 1901, a period of painstaking work marked by the discovery of the House of the Vettii, now one of the most famous in Pompeii (VI, 15), and the House of Lucretius Fronto (V, 4). He continued to excavate the northern areas of the

The plan of a typical Pompeian house can be studied from that of the House of the Centenary, as it was reconstructed in 1903 by Jules-Léon Chifflot. It was made up of two basic elements: a native Italian-style house based around an atrium, and a Hellenistic house around a peristyle. A narrow corridor (*fauces*) led from the entrance to the atrium at the lower left where the roof sloped down on all sides toward an opening in the center (*compluvium*). For a long while, it was in the main atrium—here, there is also a secondary atrium—that the household gathered for meals, work, and rest. But it was an uncomfortable room, blackened by smoke (hence the name: from *ater*, black), and it was soon reduced to the role of providing a source of light and fresh air. Opening off the atrium, opposite the entrance, was a large room (*tablinum*) flanked by two adjoining rooms (*alae*). Originally a dining room and bedroom, the *tablinum* came to be used simply as a reception room, giving access to the peristyle garden beyond, around which were arranged the bedrooms, the dining room (*triclinium*), and another reception room (*oecus*).

HELLE·0.03·P·M   POMPEI · MAISON · DV · C

RESTAVRATION
ECHELLE · 0.03 · P·M   POMPEI · MAISON · D

ENAIRE · RESTAVRATION

ENTENAIRE

Under the influence of the Hellenistic house, rooms gradually became specialized along more rational and aesthetically satisfying lines, as the service quarters were moved further away from the fine reception rooms. An architectural innovation that had an impact throughout the city was the introduction of large windows into rooms looking out onto porticoes or the garden. Above: longitudinal section of the House of the Centenary; left: transverse section, between the two atriums.

city and Regions V and VI. Towers X and XI of the outer wall were found, and behind the basilica were discovered the remains of a temple dedicated to Venus Pompeiana, the tutelary goddess of the city. A superficial investigation was made of the Temple of Jupiter and the Temple of Apollo, but the main focus of attention shifted toward the surrounding countryside, the suburb called Pagus Augustus Felix Suburbanus, and private villas, like the Villa of the Mysteries. De Petra was above all responsible for the restoration of roofs, the covering of atria and peristyles, and the careful recreation of the inner gardens of certain houses—essential elements in restoring life and color to the city.

Between 1901 and 1905 the historian Ettore País continued work on the northern quarters between Region V (*insulae* 3 and 4) and Region VI (*insulae* 15 and 16), thus completing the excavation of areas adjoining the Via Stabiana and Via di Nola. He also discovered what remained of the Vesuvian Gate and of the water tower that had once supplied the entire city.

As Archaeologist Succeeded Archaeologist, the Work Became Increasingly Systematic

With the exception of a few tombs uncovered by the Vesuvian Gate and the Nolan Gate, no major finds mark the next directorship, that of Antonio Sogliano (1905–10). He devoted himself primarily to restoring the Corinthian *oecus* of the House of the Silver Wedding, the peristyle of the House of the Golden Cupids (VI, 17), and the balcony of the Lupanar. His primary concern was for the conservation of Pompeii, and he perfected a wide range of technical measures for this purpose, many of which are still in use today.

Vittorio Spinazzola (1910–24) vigorously pursued a program of work that was even more systematic than those that had preceded it. First, he proposed abandoning the excavation of the northern quarters of the city completely, in favor of the southern quarters. His aim was to link the city center with the amphitheater and to follow the Via dell'Abbondanza as far as the

The House of Lucretius Fronto was excavated under Giulio de Petra in 1900. Methods had not progressed significantly since the previous century; workmen still carried the earth away in baskets before emptying it into horse-drawn carts. They worked down through the surface layer of ash toward the interior of the house, restoring the structure as they went. As we can see here, the stucco surface of the columns was restored with considerable care.

Sarnian Gate. This was an inspired plan, prompted by a concern with the realities of town planning, rather than the illusory satisfaction of making extraordinary discoveries; it sought to reveal the commercial life of the city through the external appearance of its main artery, rather than by simply continuing to uncover more private houses.

But this plan had its drawbacks. By confining themselves to the frontages of the buildings on either side of the road—which, in the area being excavated, was about 2000 feet long—the archaeologists not only lost the opportunity to excavate houses that were rich with promise, but were also forced to guess at the precise purpose of a shop, boutique, or building of unusual appearance by interpreting the paintings, election posters, and graffiti that covered their facades. In addition, they had to protect the facades from the weight of the earth that lay behind them. Spinazzola therefore found it impossible to stick to his original plan, and when he came upon buildings of particular interest, he decided to strike out into the *insula*, excavating as far as the alley behind. And so, for the first 1300 feet the excavations trace an irregular pattern, widening and contracting like the banks of a river; even today this uneven appearance remains.

Nevertheless, there were considerable advantages for the excavator in following a single street; it resulted in a unified restoration, the conservation of paintings and wall advertisements, and of shop furnishings. All this revealed a Pompeii that had been scarcely dreamed of and which aroused the enthusiasm of all those who visited the site.

Working by this method, Spinazzola discovered the Fullonica Stephani (I, 6), an industrial enterprise within a private house, and the *thermopolium*, or inn, of Asellina (IX, 11). He chose to excavate the houses that seemed most wealthy: the House of Paquius Proculus (I, 7), the House of the Cryptoporticus (I, 6), the House of

The Via dell' Abbondanza links the forum with the Sarnian Gate and, thus, with the amphitheater. This photograph, taken in 1910, illustrates the criticisms that can be made of Spinazzola's methods. Although the work initially appeared impressive, the facades had to be shored up to prevent them from collapsing.

Lucius Ceius Secundus (I, 6), the House of Trebius
Valens (III, 2) and that of Loreius Tiburtinus (II, 5); he
also uncovered the House of the Moralist (V, 1). But his
name remains most closely associated with the
excavation of the Via dell'Abbondanza.

Under the "regime" of Amedeo Maiuri
(1924–61), the excavations at Pompeii
took a new direction and acquired an
added dimension. Maiuri must above all
be credited with perfecting our knowledge of the history of the city through
more extensive and more carefully conducted excavations. It is with him that
we enter the age of scientific archaeology,
which alone can preserve the miracle of
Pompeii. His successors, A. de Franciscis,
F. Zevi, and I. Cerulli have followed the
same path.

The Pompeian Miracle

An average city inhabited by average people, Pompeii
would have achieved a comfortable mediocrity and
passed peacefully into the silence of history, had the
sudden catastrophe of the volcanic eruption not wiped
it from the world of the living.

Frozen for centuries, messages about the daily life of
the Pompeian people are still there for us to read, if we
can decipher them. In Pompeii the ancient world speaks
to us directly, touches us through the thousands of
events of an apparently normal, everyday world. The
workmen are busy mixing plaster to cover the
cryptoporticus of the Villa of the Mysteries; the altar
tables are prepared for the priests of Isis.

Pompeii is so moving and fascinating because we
rediscover there the occupations, feelings, dreams, and
fantasies of men and women who seem so close to us, so
full of life. The real miracle of Pompeii lies in the fact
that, so many centuries after its disastrous fate, it can
vividly conjure up the joys and sorrows, hopes and fears
of a small provincial city that entered the annals of
history in spite of itself. Pompeii is not the privileged
domain of specialists; it belongs to all of humanity.

Amedeo Maiuri casts
an excited eye over
the Venus of the Shell, a
magnificent mural found
in the House of Julia
Felix. It was uncovered
for the second time in
1952–3.

The city revealed to us by the excavations has a long history. How did it develop from a small community of fishermen and farmers in the 10th century B.C. into the flourishing city of twenty thousand inhabitants that was buried beneath the ash on 24 August 79?

CHAPTER II
LIFE IN POMPEII

Before the eruption of 79, on 5 February 62, a violent earthquake destroyed a triumphal arch and the Temple of the Capitoline Triad, with its colonnaded portico.

The Varied Saga of Occupying Forces: Oscans, Greeks, Etruscans, Samnites, Romans

The original village, inhabited by the Oscans, a native Italian people, was built on a steep volcanic ridge produced by a prehistoric lava flow. It probably lay at the heart of Regions VII and VIII (see pp. 46–7), where the irregular pattern of the roads, which survived all later occupations, clearly illustrates the primitive nature of the settlement.

In the 6th century B.C. the Greeks settled here, taking advantage of the site's excellent strategic position on an important maritime trade route. They built a Doric temple on a spur of land overlooking the valley of the river Sarno and the sea, and introduced the cult of Apollo. For the Greeks, however, Pompeii was only an outpost, allowing them to maintain control of the port and sea outlets from the hinterland, rather than a permanent settlement.

At some point between 524 and 474 B.C., the Etruscans occupied the town, though they left no trace of any specific building work. From 474 to 424 B.C., Pompeii again experienced strong Greek influence; temples were restored, the town was fortified by a surrounding wall, and enlarged with the construction of Region VI. This followed the principles of the architect of Piraeus, Hippodamus of Miletus, in that it was laid out according to a regular geometric grid, with numerous roads providing access and communication.

The Osco-Greek town was next brutally conquered by the Samnites, rough mountain dwellers from the Abruzzi and Calabria, who in 424 B.C. swept down on the Greek "colonies" on the coast. The Samnites who settled on the coastal plains became known as *Campani*, and so Pompeii became a Campanian town; the people adopted the Oscan tongue once more, as it was common to both the original occupants of the town and the new arrivals. Although the Romans subjected the Samnites who had

The Oscan alphabet (below left) included some signs that stood for letters and others that stood for syllables. The Oscan language was spoken by all Pompeians until the creation of the Roman colony and continued in use among the general population for a good while afterward.

Pompeii retained certain traces of the Greek period of occupation. The cult of Apollo, for example, celebrated during the Archaic period (7th century B.C.) under the influence of the maritime empire of Cumae, survived the Etruscan occupation (524–474 B.C.). It was adopted by the Oscans and Campanians, and later, of course, by the Romans. The Temple of Apollo was built on rising ground, dominating the main routes through the city. It is seen here as reconstructed by the Romans. On the left is the podium of the temple itself, where the cult statue stood, and on the right is a colonnaded courtyard made of tufa and stucco. On a level with the fifth column stands a Herm surmounted by a marble bust of Mercury.

CAPUAN Gate

VESUVIAN Necropolis Gate

Necropolis

HERCULANEUM Gate

REG. V

Hse of the Ara Massima

Hse of Lucretius F

Hse of

Hse of Meleager

9 11

15 16

Hse of the Centaur

Hse of the Golden Cupids Hse of the Moralist

Hse of the Silver Wedding

3

1 5

Hse of the Surgeon

REG. VI

Hse of the Vettii

Hse of the Labyrinth

Hse of Caecilius Jucundus

2

Hse of the Amazons

7

1

Via di Nola

8

Hse Cen

Hse of Sallust

12 13 14

2

5

3 8

Hse of Pansa

10

Hse of the Faun

Hse of the Anchor

Via della Fortuna

3

Central Baths

4

Hse of M. Lucretius

3

6

6

Hse of the Tragic Poet

Temple of Fortuna Augusta

Bakery of Terentius Proculus

Bakery

4

Via delle Terme

Forum Baths

4

2

1

6 5

Via degli Augustali

Inn of Sittius

2

Temple of the Capitoline Triad

Market

REG. VII 12

Via del Balcone pensile

1

Hse of Casca Lon

7

Sanctuary of the Lares Temple of Vespasian

9 10 11

Stabian Baths

4

15

Temple of Apollo

Building of Eumachia

Hse of the Skeleton

13 14

Hse of Cornelius Rufus

1

Forum

Via dell'Abbondanza

Hse of the Holconii

MARINE Gate

8

Comitium

5 6

Via del Tempio di Isi

Te M

Via Marina

Basilica

2 3

REG. VIII

Samnite palaestra

Temple of Isis

Museum Temple of Venus

1

Vico della Regina

Triangular Forum

Large theatre

O

Doric temple

Gladiators' barracks

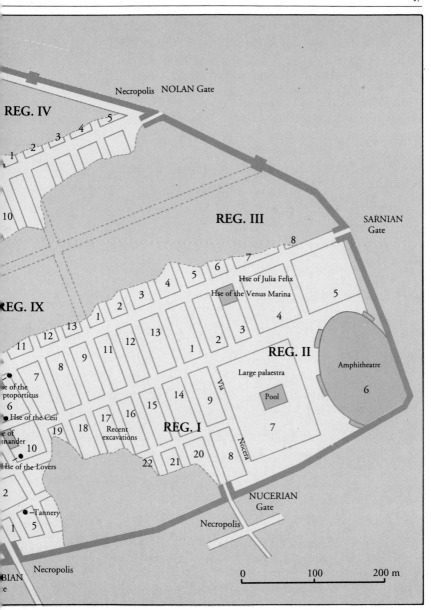

REG. IV

Necropolis   NOLAN Gate

SARNIAN
Gate

REG. III

8

7

6

5

Hse of Julia Felix

Hse of the Venus Marina

5

REG. IX

4

3

2

1

13

12

11

10

13

12

11

1

2

3

4

5

6

7

8

9

10

19

18

17

16

15

14

9

Recent
excavations

REG. I

22 21 20 8

REG. II

Large palaestra

Pool

Amphitheatre

6

7

Via Nocera

Hse of the
ptoporticus

Hse of the Ceii

se of
:hander

Hse of the Lovers

2

1 5

Tannery

NUCERIAN
Gate

Necropolis

Necropolis

BIAN

0   100   200 m

remained in their mountainous homeland to fierce military attack, they formed an alliance with the Campani. Neither Pyrrhus, king of Epirus, in c. 280 B.C., nor Hannibal in 216 B.C.—to whom all the other cities of Campania swore allegiance—could shake Pompeii's loyalty to Rome.

As a defense against its turbulent neighbors and a guarantee of independence from Rome, Pompeii

remained throughout this period a fortified city. Between 424 and 89 B.C. it was surrounded with an increasingly solid system of fortifications: two parallel walls of black tufa and limestone, buttressed by an *agger*, or earth mound, with twelve square towers straddling the ramparts. From north to south these fortifications were built over the old city walls, showing that the town had not expanded in that direction, though it had developed considerably in the whole of the eastern sector. The 10,000 feet of urban perimeter that we see today were therefore established by the

B etween the Herculaneum Gate and the Vesuvian Gate —shown here, in the background—three towers, including this one, Tower X, punctuate the Samnite fortifications.

Samnites. This impressive defensive wall defined the city's limits, beyond which lay the burial grounds.

The Samnites also established the main arteries of the city; their aim was to link the Triangular Forum and its complex of monuments with the civil forum by the present-day Via del Tempio di Iside and the Via dei Teatri, while the Via Stabiana (or Via Pompeiana, as it is called in an inscription) crossed the city from north to south, continuing by a bridge over the river Sarno as far as the town of Stabiae.

In March 90 B.C. the Samnite towns rose up against Rome, and this time Pompeii joined the rebels. The war against the "allies" under the leadership of Sulla proved difficult and prolonged. Pompeii was besieged, and its walls were bombarded with huge stone balls marked with the name of Sulla; the tufa still bears their indelible imprint. Between summer 90 and autumn 89 B.C., the city succumbed. Thereafter Pompeii was Roman but at peace, a situation that was to last until that fateful day in 79.

Monumental Districts, Residential Districts

Rome brought no great changes, as far as town planning was concerned; the Roman way of life was introduced into districts that owed their essentially monumental or residential character to the Samnite era, even after they had undergone reconstruction or restoration (especially after the earthquake of 62).

It was in the forum, which was at once the religious, political, and commercial center, that the heart of the Roman colony lay. The Temple of the Capitoline Triad (or Temple of Jupiter), the Temple of the Lares, and the Temple of Vespasian were all to be found here. Political matters were dealt with in the Curia and in the offices of the magistrates, while the market (*macellum*), the

The roadbed was made up of tightly packed chalk or trachyte blocks. When it rained, pedestrians could keep their feet dry by crossing on large stepping-stones, which had space between them for the passage of cart wheels (top).

building of Eumachia, the wool and cloth market, and the *mensa ponderaria,* or office of weights and measures, represented the commercial center of the city.

The old Triangular Forum now became part of the theater quarter, acting as a foyer to the large theater

The Vico di Mercurio (left) leads from Tower XI to the forum. The so-called Arch of Caligula is in the background. In the foreground are the Houses of Meleager and of the Centaur.

and offering an area to stroll in during the intermission. Also nearby were the Samnite *palaestra,* or sports ground, the Temple of Isis, and the Temple of Jupiter Meilichios, so this part of the town combined both religious and athletic functions. The area around the amphitheater, to the southeast, included a second, larger *palaestra.* This was the most spacious quarter of the city, where crowds of spectators could enjoy the shade of the plane trees, sampling the many delicacies that were on sale there.

Virtually all the remaining

In the southwest corner of the forum lies the basilica, with its three vast aisles. Justice was dispensed from the tribunal that stands at the end of the central nave (above). The raised platform of the tribunal is ornamented with six Corinthian pillars, topped by a smaller colonnade with a decorative pediment.

The Pompeian House: Architectural Mastery

The architect François Mazois (see p. 25) executed fine reconstruction drawings showing every detail of the roof and *compluvium* of a typical atrium (opposite, above: view from above and elevation). The *impluvium* at floor level would have corresponded with the open square above formed by the four slopes of the roof. The system of roof trusses, beams, and rafters is clearly illustrated (opposite, below), together with the arrangement of flat edging tiles (*tegulae*) and rounded tiles, which concealed the joins (*imbrices*). In summer the Pompeians dined in the open air, just as they do today, taking their couches out under the peristyle or into the garden. To avoid having to carry around such heavy pieces of furniture, carved stone couches were often placed in the garden around a stone table. Close by, a small shrine was provided for libations. The section and schematic view (left) show a particularly simple *triclinium*, with no arbor to offer shade or fountain to cool the air.

Decorative Schemes: Painting Set Free

The wealthy citizens of Pompeii used paintings to create an "imaginary museum" within their own homes; these decorative schemes therefore help us to penetrate their spiritual lives and to assess their tastes. There is no longer any secret about how Pompeian paintings were executed; pigments were mixed in a solution of lime and soap, with a little added wax, then the finished painting was burnished (using a metal trowel, a marble or glass cylinder, or a special polishing stone), and buffed with a clean cloth. In one of the dining rooms of the House of the Vettii (opposite) panels depict mythological subjects. The elaborate architectural vistas are typical of the fourth style of wall painting in Pompeii. In the third style (above left) the architectural elements are merely ornamental, creating the impression of a closed recess; the landscape looks more like a painting than a realistic view through a window into space. The still life (below left) celebrates a taste for beautifully crafted objects, displaying a collection of silver worthy of the House of Menander.

Pompeian Gardens: the Taming of Nature

The increasing amount of space devoted to gardens corresponds to the Romans' love of nature. A garden provided greenery and coolness, but it was also charged with dreams; some Pompeians sought to emulate the palace gardens of the great Hellenistic princes. Flowering plants, plane and cypress trees, ivy, bay, and oleander were combined to create effects worthy of a large park, while the careful arrangement of clumps of trees and flower borders underlined the Pompeians' desire to introduce an architectural structure into their gardens. Through paintings, this taste for greenery and for formality was continued into the house itself. In both the frieze above and the mural below, wooden balustrades made of interwoven laths define semicircular and rectangular alcoves, which create the illusion of a series of planes receding into depth. By means of these alcoves, the painter introduces into the garden, at regular intervals, fountains, ceramic vases, and birds, which perch on the wooden arbor or strut about on the lawn.

districts of the city were residential, and their development during the Roman period is punctuated by the construction of the public baths that were such an essential part of daily life in Pompeii. The oldest of these, the Stabian Baths, had been built in the Samnite period; but the Forum Baths date from the establishment of the Roman colony, and the Central Baths were still under construction at the time of the eruption. They all stand on main roads, at the edge of the old Oscan center, where the winding streets in the shadow of the Lupanar were the haunt of prostitutes.

Certain streets, where *thermopolia* and taverns were interspersed with shops, had a more commercial flavor. And, surprisingly, in the heart of the city there remained a semi-rustic quarter (in Region I), where several summer couches lay amid rural gardens; there was even a vineyard where wine could be purchased. As an active, commercial city, Pompeii retained a rustic character that was much appreciated by lovers of good food and fine wines.

When He Created the Colony in 80 B.C., Sulla Made Pompeii a Mini-Rome Responsible for Its Own Internal Affairs

Supreme authority in Pompeii rested with the two *duoviri*, who made legal pronouncements and were responsible for administering public funds and presiding over the meetings of the town council. Below them, two other magistrates, or *aediles*, were in charge of many of the less important administrative tasks, such as road maintenance, the supervision of the markets, and organization of the police. Each of these officials had a building on the forum for his offices and records. The Curia, also on the forum, was the seat of the municipal council, which was made up of one hundred *decuriones*, most of whom were former magistrates.

"Fuscus and Vaccula Advise You to Vote for A. Vettius Firmus, Candidate for the Aedileship"

In July of each year Pompeians voted for the municipal magistrates. As early as the spring, election fever hit

The vast houses belonging to important Pompeians always contained the essential garden, like this one in the House of the Faun, where clumps of bushes blend with the ornamental pools and niches for sacred statues.

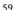

the city. Walls were covered in posters painted in red or black. As there were no areas reserved specifically for posters, citizens would also express their personal support for a particular candidate by devoting part of the front of their house to him. The inhabitants of a quarter *(vicini)* would often employ advertising

Groups of neighbors would have their names inscribed on the house of an electoral candidate in red letters. Here they express their support for Lucretius Fronto and Caius Julius Polybius, whom they judge worthy of the *res publica*, the civic community, and of the office of *duovir*, or magistrate.

companies to whitewash the walls, frequently working right through the night to erase the inscriptions of the previous year.

In contrast to present-day political practice, it was not considered appropriate for the candidate himself to call for votes; others sought them on his behalf by presenting him as the man most worthy of the office. There were no elaborate professions of faith, no boasts about a brilliant career, no promises to support a public building program, implement tax cuts, or improve the quality of the roads; all that mattered was the testimony of others to the candidate's good moral character.

This explains why one important citizen running for office, Caius Julius Polybius, enraged by the fact that Cuculla and Zmyrina, two prostitutes at his local bar, had declared their support for him, demanded that their inscriptions be erased; clearly, to be sponsored by people of such ill repute could do his cause no good at all.

Although women could neither run for office nor vote,

At the time of the Pompeian catastrophe, the Jewish communities started the rumor that the eruption of Vesuvius was divine vengeance for the destruction Titus (above) had wrought on the Temple of Jerusalem eight years earlier.

they nevertheless played an active role in the election campaigns, which shed fascinating light on relationships between neighbors, on ties of interdependence, and on the influence of corporate and religious bodies on the political process.

Though Pompeii Was Self-Governing in Municipal Matters, It Was Still Subject to Imperial Decree

Once elected, the magistrates would never venture to involve themselves in broader political issues or to question the objectives defined in Rome by the emperor and his ministers. Their horizon was limited to the administration of municipal affairs, the most urgent concern after the earthquake of 62 being the reconstruction of the city. With the arrival of each new emperor, the city displayed its loyalty; the imperial cult was celebrated annually by a *flamen*, or special priest, and there were increasing numbers of shrines to the Augustan Virtues.

In general, Rome interfered little in the internal affairs of Pompeii, except when public order was threatened. In 59, for example, when a brawl erupted in the amphitheater between people from Pompeii and Nocera (see pp. 108–9), the *duoviri* then in office, the brothers Grosphi, were dismissed; two replacements were selected, and Nero appointed a law-giving prefect (*iure dicundo*) to supervise them. The emperor also went so far as to suspend the games, though he would reinstate them a little later to universal joy, thereby underlining his omnipotence and reinforcing his popularity.

Another imperial intervention occurred when Vespasian dispatched T. Suedius Clemens to restore order to the tax registers and to reclaim city land that had been appropriated by corrupt entrepreneurs. At no point did the Pompeians consider this an unacceptable attack on their autonomy; on the contrary, through this "most holy" judge, they rendered homage to his noble master.

Constructed during the closing years of the 1st century B.C. by Marcus Tullius, the Temple of Fortuna Augusta, which stands to the north of the forum on the Via del Foro, imitated the structure of the Temple of the Capitoline Triad, with two flights of steps—one on either side of the central altar—leading to a platform at the foot of the podium. Eight columns with Corinthian capitals, four of them forming the facade, support the portico in front of the *cella*. The statue of Fortuna Augusta, which stood on a pedestal at the back of the sanctuary, reminded the worshipers that the emperor brought them good luck and thus ensured the happiness of every Pompeian citizen.

How did the people of Pompeii earn a living? Was the town full of individuals who, attracted by the mild climate and beautiful countryside of Campania, had retired to Pompeii with their lifetime's savings? Or did they work hard, struggling, after the earthquake of 62, to confront the misfortune that had struck rich and poor alike?

CHAPTER III
EARNING A LIVING

By this point bread was no longer made at home; Pompeians bought it each day from the bakery, a sign of the development of small-scale trade. Mercury, god of commerce, appeared everywhere.

Lucrum gaudium, "profit is joy": so runs the motto inscribed around the edge of the *impluvium* in a modest house belonging to a wood-turner. Elsewhere, in the entrance hall of a more wealthy dwelling owned by the two important citizens Siricus and Numerianus, a mosaic inscription again pays tribute to profit: *salve lucrum.* Mercury, the god of commerce, is omnipresent, whether on the sales counter of an inn or on the wall of a fulling mill.

The Propertied Classes: Profit from the Land

Campania has always been an agricultural paradise. The fertile slopes of Vesuvius were dotted with estates where, between rows of vines and olive trees, cereals, vegetables, and animal fodder were grown. The cultivation of spelt, a variety of durum wheat, enabled farmers to obtain two harvests a year, which helped to enrich the owners of wine-producing properties like the Villa of the Mysteries; here, a wine press and cellars, where round-bellied earthenware jars (*dolia*) held the harvests of wine and oil, point to production of a very high quality. The rearing of animals also flourished. Eumachia, the rich owner of a building on the forum, married a certain Numistrius, the owner of pastures and sheep. In a pen at his villa pigs and sheep were guarded by dogs.

The city itself required what was virtually a market-garden suburb to keep it supplied with food; the gardens of Pompeii (*horti pompeiani*) are still famous today for their onions and herbs, as well as for their honey, which was used to sweeten the wine.

Money earned through the land, concentrated in the hands of a few important individuals, brought political influence as well as economic power. Most of the members of the decurion council were freeborn wealthy landowners.

Bread and *Garum*: the Two Major Food Industries

Basic foodstuffs were mainly produced by small tradesmen and, occasionally, by the wealthy owners of the agricultural estates. Bakeries can be identified from

This blue amphora still contained wine when it was discovered in a tomb. It is decorated with pastoral and Bacchic scenes, divided by elegantly curling vine tendrils. For the people of Pompeii, wine was the drink of immortality.

This round loaf, found in an oven, was divided into eight portions—a tradition carried on in Campania to the present day.

their millstones of grey-black tufa, which were turned by slaves with the aid of a wooden handle (*mola trusatilis*), or by a horse or donkey led by a slave (*mola asinaria*). The baker kneaded the dough, baked the bread in an elaborate oven, and sold it in the adjoining shop; pastry chefs operated from smaller premises where they stored their many cake molds.

Garum, which Seneca hated on account of its foul smell, was a sauce which must have resembled the

L ava millstones are set up ready for use in the courtyard of this bread factory. In the foreground stands the rotating, funnel-shaped *catillus*, which held the grain. In the background is the oven.

Vietnamese *nuoc-mam*, made of dried fish with salt added as a preservative. Its production was generally the monopoly of prosperous families, such as the Umbricii, because of the amount of initial investment required. A. Umbricius Scaurus, *duovir* under Claudius, supplied *garum* wholesale to a variety of retail outlets. The quality depended on the type of fish used: tuna, mackerel, and moray eel for the more delicate varieties, and anchovies for *garum* intended for poor men and slaves.

Spinners, Fullers, and Dyers

Sheep breeding supplied a flourishing wool industry, controlled once again by the top families, which employed a whole army of craftspeople. The fine building of Eumachia on the forum, where raw wool and finished cloth were probably sold, symbolizes the importance of the industry.

Once it had been washed, degreased, and carded, the wool was sent to the spinners. The woolen threads were then stretched over a vertical or horizontal loom,

ready for weaving. Spinning and weaving were often carried out by the female slaves of a household, the cloth being sent to be treated by the fullers and dyers. The fulling process was carried out by the *coactiliarii*, who trod the finished cloth in a mixture of fuller's earth, potash, soda, and urine. Once it had been rinsed, dried, brushed, and bleached with sulphur or dyed in bright colors, such as purple or saffron yellow, it was ready to go on sale. Other workshops had the job of putting new life into old cloth by changing its color. M. Vecilius Verecundus, one of the great fulling-mill owners, was an eminent member of the industrial bourgeoisie in Pompeii.

A t the dyeing workshop of M. Vecilius Verecundus (above left) the workers first plunge the cloth into vats of dye, then hold it up to judge the quality of the result.

The Concentration of Wealth

After the earthquake of 62 the most urgent task was to reconstruct the city, and in order to produce sufficient quantities of tiles and bricks, the very profitable export of wine and *garum* was stepped up. Increasing numbers of amphorae had to be manufactured for the export of these products, and as the wine and *garum* producers also tended to own the kilns, as well as the brick and tile factories essential for rebuilding, wealth gradually became increasingly concentrated in the hands of a fortunate few.

Trade was booming: Pompeian landowners exported

To raise the tangled nap of the cloth, the workman on the left brushes it with an instrument to which thistles, thorns, and prickles are affixed. The bell-shaped wicker frame on the right is designed to support the lengths of fabric while they are drying or being bleached with sulfur. The second workman carries a hot dish containing the burning sulfur.

their agricultural surpluses, while products arrived from overseas via the *Sarnus pompeianus*, the river Sarno. Thanks to its port, Pompeii was classified as an entrepôt, an intermediate center of trade. Pictures of ships, graffiti, and mosaic emblems such as anchors often indicate the homes of shipowners. Pompeian wine was exported to Gaul from as early as the 1st century B.C., and Pompeian tiles have been found as far away as Dalmatia. Pompeian traders wove a complex network to the Orient, Egypt, Africa, and even Asia, their caravans reaching as far afield as the ports of Syria and Palestine, and, via the Red Sea and the canal of Nechao II, Alexandria, Egypt.

The Merchant Bankers of Pompeii

To get an idea of the range of these Pompeian fortunes we can study the accounts that have been discovered in certain houses. For example, on 3 and 5 July 1875 more than 150 writing tablets were unearthed in the house of the merchant banker L. Caecilius Jucundus, on the eastern side of the Via Stabiana. The tablets had originally been covered with a thin film of wax—hence their name, *tabulae ceratae*—and, as they still bore the marks made with the point of a stylus, it was possible to read what had been written on them. They were receipts (*apochae*) for the years 52 to 62, drawn up by Jucundus himself, by his secretary, or occasionally by the person who had just received the loan. Jucundus acted as a broker, lending capital to merchants in return for a fee. The amounts involved vary between 342 and 38,079 sesterces, an average of 8502 sesterces per transaction, which indicates quite considerable fortunes. Even so, the banker was only among the fairly well-off families of the city, and was not a member of Pompeii's true oligarchy.

This bronze portrait bust of Lucius Caecilius Jucundus, the most famous banker in Pompeii, was found in the atrium of his house. He has the face of a realist, with a hint of provincial roughness, the ironic expression of his eyes reflecting the businessperson's astute intelligence.

The Wealth of Pompeians Can Also Be Assessed from the Treasures They Snatched Up as They Fled from the Rain of Ash

These amounts of money, which must correspond to what the average citizen happened to have readily available in cash, range from about 3000 to 10,000 sesterces. Twenty-six of them represent large sums of money: the highest was 9448 sesterces; six of the finds were over 4000; and the remainder were somewhere between 1000 and 4000 sesterces. These were plainly wealthy citizens.

In about sixty other cases the average amount was approximately 200 sesterces. Whether they involve significant sums or small change —the poor had on them only a few copper coins ("asses") to cover the cost of food—the range of these finds clearly indicates the scale of incomes in Pompeii.

The Workers: Laborers, Employees, and Shopkeepers

First, there were those whose only capital was their hands. Slaves or freedmen, they carried out work in the fields, tending the vines, picking grapes, plowing, harvesting, hay making, caring for the orchards, and growing vegetables.

Other workers were employed in the bakeries and around the vats of *garum* or the fulling tanks, amid the sickening smells of the tanneries. A vast industrial

For keeping his accounts, the banker used a rigid wooden tablet covered with a thin film of wax, and a folding tablet prepared in the same way, in which he recorded each business transaction. The circular box, or *capsa*, was used to store rolls of papyrus.

Pieces of gold and silver were discovered in this silver purse, carried by a chain, which was found in the wealthy House of Menander.

These putti, or cupids, in the House of the Vettii symbolize the various activities of the Pompeian guilds. On the far left the pharmacist cupid is shaking a prepared medicine in a glass retort. Dangerous products are stored in the medicine cabinet behind him. Above left: the silversmith cupid is busy fashioning a piece of jewelry; a pair of Roman scales and a smaller assay balance indicate the precision with which precious metals had to be weighed. A blacksmith cupid introduces his tongs into the fierce flames of the forge, below left, while blowing through some form of pipe to heat up the embers. On the right another cupid is putting the finishing touches on a large round dish made of gold.

workforce manufactured a whole variety of bronze and silver objects, from safes to mirrors and brazier stands, from high-precision metalwork for architectural, surveying, and surgical instruments, to jewelry that would satisfy even the most demanding customer.

At the market on the forum, along the sidewalks and in the shade of the plane trees in the square near the amphitheater, there swarmed crowds of traders, shoe and fabric sellers, peddlers of pottery, mule-drivers, and porters. Advertisers, doctors, and painters could also be found there, alongside musicians and schoolteachers. Together they constituted what today would be called the service industries.

And what of the unemployed? Only rarely were people truly unemployed; there was always some work to be found—seasonal work, at least, with all the hay making, harvesting, and grape picking that went on in the large estates around the city. And, of course, every time a ship came into the Pompeian port on the river Sarnus manpower was required to unload its cargo. Above all, after the earthquake of 62, the task of reconstructing the city ensured plenty of work for everyone.

Every ancient Mediterranean city also had its share of beggars who survived on public charity. It seems that in Pompeii the blind and disabled did not starve to death. There was always a small coin, a crust of bread, or a bowl of stew to help them out, to supply their basic needs.

The great variety of surgical instruments —needles, speculum, scalpel, forceps, scissors—illustrates the development of medical science during the 1st century A.D. Like the brazier (left), they testify to the high quality and precision of Pompeian metalwork.

An artisan (right) strikes the chisel with a mallet in order to make notches in a piece of wood. Carpenters played a vital role in the construction of all new buildings, either on an individual basis or as members of organized professional bodies.

C harity eased the
misery of the poor
and the handicapped. A
wealthy woman
accompanied by a servant
offers a coin to a blind
man (left).

A market was held each week under the portico of the forum, which was decorated with garlands of flowers for the occasion (left). The stalls were set out at pavement level. A shoemaker on the right shows off his wares to two seated female customers, while others wait their turn. On the left, an elderly man appears to have fallen asleep over the take-out meals he is offering for sale; large jars contain the stews and sauces.

A City Where Social Harmony Reigned

In this population, estimated at 20,000 inhabitants (8000 slaves and 12,000 freedmen, of whom 4200 were adults), rich and poor lived happily side by side, just as the Greeks, Etruscans, Oscans, and Romans had done down through the centuries. The city experienced no interclass strife or racial discrimination; slaves and freedmen shared in the fortunes of their masters, and relationships of economic interdependence enabled everyone to earn their daily bread. And all the more easily, since basic foodstuffs were cheaper in Pompeii than in many other cities of the empire (see pp. 184–5).

Women of the classical world had achieved relative emancipation long before the 1st century A.D. They no longer lived cloistered lives in the *gynaeceum*, subject to their husband's will. They mingled with the crowds in the forum, participating in all the hustle and bustle of street life. Many Pompeian women even declared themselves the equal of men.

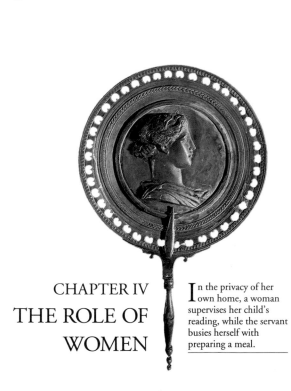

CHAPTER IV

THE ROLE OF WOMEN

In the privacy of her own home, a woman supervises her child's reading, while the servant busies herself with preparing a meal.

The colonnade around the forum, where vendors have set up their stalls on the pavement, is festooned with brightly colored garlands. A shoemaker sings the praises of his wares to two customers seated in front of him on a bench. A wealthy lady, accompanied by her slave, has just given alms to a blind beggar dressed in rags. The frescoes in the House of Julia Felix (pp. 74–5) show clearly that women were present in the streets as well as in the houses of Pompeii.

Once Upon a Time There Was a Future Empress

The life of Sabina Poppaea begins like a fairy tale. She was born into a rich Pompeian family who owned two sumptuously appointed houses: the House of the Golden Cupids, whose peristyle is decorated with several theatrical masks, and the House of Menander, where 118 pieces of silverware were discovered. Sabina was beautiful, and well aware of it. Her fellow citizens made no secret of their admiration for her; one wall bears the words: "May you blossom forever, Sabina, preserve your beauty and your maidenhood for many years."

But she paid no heed to this advice, sacrificing her virtue to the emperor Nero, who married her in 62. This was the very year in which an earthquake destroyed her hometown, and Poppaea must surely have prevailed upon her husband to help the townspeople, just as she later asked him to authorize the people of Pompeii to hold gladiatorial contests; Nero had imposed a ban on the games in 59 to punish the Pompeians for having massacred their neighbors from Nocera in the arena. Permission was granted, and

The wealthy and charming Sabina Poppaea, who had property in Pompeii itself, also owned a sumptuously decorated country villa (right), recently discovered at Oplontis (Torre Annunziata).

This gold *bulla*, or amulet (above left), and a bracelet in the shape of a snake may have been part of Poppaea's personal collection of jewelry.

the Pompeians were overjoyed. They expressed their excitement by writing on the walls of their city graffiti that were found centuries later: "Three cheers for imperial decrees; three cheers for the decisions of the emperor and empress. Long live the Empress Poppaea." A few years later they remembered the emperor's gesture and held games to celebrate Nero's fortunate escape from the Naples earthquake of A.D. 64.

Not Even a Rich Landowner like Julia Felix Could Escape the Effects of an Earthquake

The House of Julia Felix occupied a whole *insula*, or block. Vast, beautiful, and magnificently decorated, this residence bears witness to the wealth and good taste of its owner.

As in all Pompeian houses, the rooms were arranged around an interior garden where fountains murmured and decorative plants complemented the architecture. The peristyle was made up of slim, fluted marble pilasters crowned by Corinthian capitals. It framed the entrance to the dining room, the finest room in the house, which was richly furnished with marble couches for the guests. The end wall was covered with stones to

These paintings in the House of Julia Felix are not mere exercises in illusionism, but rather proclamations of a taste for elegant objects, for succulent fruits that evoke the glorious riches of Pompeian agriculture. On the shelf stand a bronze mortar with a long-handled spoon, a plate of large eggs, and a pewter *oenochoe*, or wine jug; four thrushes and a fringed cloth are hanging on the wall. A small amphora containing some precious old wine leans against the shelf.

create the effect of a nymph's grotto, and water trickled softly onto the marble steps of a fountain, creating a wonderful freshness. Yet Julia Felix was not satisfied with such dazzling luxury; in her garden she preferred to relax in a summer *triclinium* that was more rustic in character, the carved beds and table painted in bright colors. Every room in the house was painted with scenes taken from life, which evoked the noise and bustle of the forum, or with still lifes, in which the artists created an illusion of depth from arrangements of ordinary domestic objects, skillfully

This crystal bowl overflows with fruit; apples, pears, apricots, pomegranates, and a bunch of well-ripened, dark purple grapes display their full and luscious forms. An apple has fallen from the bowl; a pomegranate has split open. Further down, a pot filled with grapes and an amphora await the pleasure of the guests.

We can perhaps imagine the real Julia Felix through the features of this noble Campanian lady, with her rounded face and plump neck set off by her straight, dark hair parted in the middle. Her expression is thoughtful, almost melancholy.

An Age of Beauty

The gods and goddesses of the classical world were very closely associated with ordinary mortals, and so in paintings it is often hard to distinguish a mythological subject from a scene of everyday life. The bodies of the three Graces (far left) express youthful awkwardness rather than sensuality, suggesting a trio of young girls surprised without their clothes rather than three striking and voluptuous goddesses. They bring a discreet charm and a hint of innocent eroticism to this pictorial common-place. Similarly, is it the goddess Flora picking flowers to make up a "divine" bouquet, or simply the lady of the house, the *domina,* wishing to decorate one of her rooms (left), as she walks through the garden, gracefully draped in a colored robe?

The Autumn of Life

Growing old was not something to look forward to in Pompeii; old women were the target of cruel caricatures by painters and mosaicists, who especially liked to portray them as characters in plays by Menander. Here, an old woman, with hollow eyes and a wrinkled face, and two younger, rather plain peasant women—probably mother and daughter—are sitting at a table, on which an incense burner and a laurel wreath lie. The old woman is about to prepare a charm; she has been asked a question and waves her hands in the air, then drinks from a goblet of wine. The young woman on the far left wrings her hands in despair, while the servant, on the right, stands quietly by. Aged fortune-tellers could turn the credulity of ordinary folk to good advantage.

using light to throw the riches of nature into high relief.

This wealthy Pompeian lady, whose whole life seems to have been devoted to the carefree enjoyment of luxury, did not escape the dramatic events that struck the city. Her house was badly shaken by the earthquake of 62. Yet she remained calm in the face of adversity and decided to pay for repairs to her home by renting part of it, which she had converted into public baths, shops, and a *thermopolium*. Julia Felix epitomizes a class of women who owed their independence to large inherited fortunes, but who did not seek to play any economic role in city life.

Eumachia, Businesswoman and Priestess, Displays Her Wealth

Another woman who occupied a position of unusual importance in Pompeian society was Eumachia. She was born into an old Pompeian family, the Eumachii, who owned vineyards and brickworks, as well as playing an important part in municipal affairs; one member of the *gens*, Lucius Eumachius Festus, had been an *aedile* (town magistrate) in 32. Eumachia was the owner of a vast edifice on the forum, on the corner of the Via dell'Abbondanza, measuring 200 x 130 feet; over the two entrances to the building an inscription reads: "Eumachia, daughter of Lucius, priestess of the people, in her own name and in that of her son Numistrius Fronto, built this entrance hall, a cryptoporticus and a portico with her own money, and dedicated them to the honor of Augustan Concord and Piety."

By chance, in the course of the excavations a statue of

Ground Plan of the Building of Eumachia

The facade opens onto the portico of the forum, while at the back the building leads into the Via dell'Abbondanza.

Longitudinal Section

1. Portico of the forum
2. Colonnade
3. Apse and statue of Livia
4. Gallery containing statue of Eumachia

Eumachia was found here, which had been erected by the corporation of the fullers, in honor of their generous patroness; this seems to confirm the assumption that the building was used as a wool market, an activity to which it would have been well suited. Tables and other fittings required by the traders could have been set up either in the open courtyard or under the colonnade, while the covered gallery, or cryptoporticus, which ran around three sides of the building, could have been locked up after hours to protect the merchandise stored there.

Quite apart from its suitability for commercial purposes, the building of Eumachia is striking for the

Cross-section

2. Colonnade framing the entrance to the apse
5. Gallery

monumentality and beauty of its architecture. The facade, consisting of a two-story colonnade, blends in with the new colonnade of the forum. The supports and lintel of the main entrance are ornamented with a superb carved marble frieze; niches in the facade and others inside the building were designed to display statues of the emperors—Tiberius and Drusus, no doubt—while inscriptions celebrate the lives of Aeneas and Romulus.

The general effect is reminiscent of the Augustan forum in Rome. Inside, a large courtyard surrounded by a two-story colonnade is terminated by an end wall with three semicircular apses; the central apse, fronted by two ornate columns, displays a statue of Concordia Augusta holding a cornucopia. The Concordia Augusta is a personification of the Empress Livia, wife of Augustus, and it celebrates the emotional union between her and her son Tiberius, after her illness of 22. By erecting this statue, Eumachia demonstrated her loyalty to the emperor and to his mother, indicating that she took their family relationship as a model in her own life. It is also possible that, as a public priestess, Eumachia celebrated the cult of this Livia-Ceres figure.

This building reveals the wealth and power of the Eumachii, as well as their pride, as can be seen from the fact that they dared to erect in Pompeii a small-scale imitation of the imperial forum. Ostentatious in life, they were no less so in death, as we can see from the impressive sepulcher that Eumachia had constructed for herself and her kin.

The Women Who Ran Businesses and Bars, or Who Worked Nearby

The wives of artisans and traders were often responsible for running the shop; in a painting of the baker Terentius Neo, the woman at his side holds a stylus and writing tablet for drawing up the accounts. In the shop of M. Vecilius Verecundus, a major manufacturer of cloth and felt, it is his wife who is shown sitting at the counter, while an elegantly dressed young man chooses a

The acanthus scrolls that decorate the lintel of the building of Eumachia are inhabited by small animals, snails, rats, and birds, reminding us of the Romans' taste for naturalism. The statue of Eumachia (below), on the other hand, reveals Greek influence.

pair of slippers from the cupboards full of merchandise that line the walls.

It was often women who ran the inns and bars, which were frequented by a somewhat coarse clientele. One of these innkeepers was Valeria Hedone, whose language was colorful and whose tone, strident; even her surname, which is Greek for "pleasure," implies a great deal about her. Shamelessly, she cries her wares: "Handsome soldier, drink here for just one as; for two you can drink better,

This woman, possibly a baker's wife, is typical of a class of ambitious women who played an important role in Pompeian life. In her hand she holds a jointed writing tablet, probably used for recording the accounts.

and for four have some really good Falernian wine."
If a brawl broke out between her dice-playing customers,
she could have the troublemakers thrown into the
street without a moment's hesitation. Close by, in a
"specialist" bar, a lady called Asellina was in charge of a
whole group of women who offered their charms for a
modest price in the winding streets of old Pompeii.

Palmyra the Oriental, Aglae the Greek, Maria the
Jewess, Zmyrina the Exotic: the names of
those who inhabited the Lupanar are
familiar to us from remaining graffiti,
which proclaim the women's various
specialities.

Pompeian Women Were Also Assistants and Domestic Workers

Though some are known to
us, the faces of many
Pompeian women

Rich Pompeian ladies
would have spent
much of their time sur-
rounded by a crowd of
servants (below), deciding
what to wear and having
their hair and makeup
done. Only a servant
would have knelt on the
floor (below right), but
this woman's pose
remains graceful none-
theless. Some women of
the period wrote poetry;
the young girl in the
roundel (right) bites the
end of her stylus as she
meditates, no doubt
searching for inspiration.

have been lost in the blank anonymity of their work. Among the working women of Pompeii were the bakery assistants Statia and Petronia, the women in the fulling mills, like Specula, who was employed to brush and shear the cloth, and all the many domestic servants, kitchen maids, and chambermaids, who revolved around the mistress of the house.

The pattern of daily life was recorded by the sundials and water clocks, or *clepsydrae*, which measured the passage of time. They fixed the hours of the working day and indicated when the tribunals were in session; they said when performances would begin at the theater, or games at the amphitheater; they measured the time for lovers' meetings, business dinners, and banquets with friends.

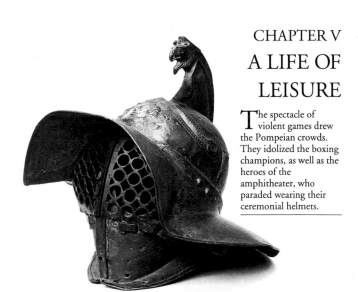

CHAPTER V
A LIFE OF LEISURE

The spectacle of violent games drew the Pompeian crowds. They idolized the boxing champions, as well as the heroes of the amphitheater, who paraded wearing their ceremonial helmets.

In the bars a favorite pastime was dice playing, but quarrels were a frequent occurrence.

These two athletes have just been proclaimed the winners of games held at the *palaestra*. The one in the foreground, his hair tied back with a headband, raises a glass vessel to celebrate his victory; the second athlete, behind him, wears a laurel wreath around his head as a mark of success.

All Pompeians tried, as far as their means would allow, to make time for *otium*—that is, leisure—the opposite of *negotium*, or work, with all its cares and worries.

Sports, the Citizens' Favorite Activity, Developed their Strength and Skills

As early as the 5th century B.C., members of the Samnite aristocracy were training at the Samnite *palaestra*, or sports ground. This was far too small for the Romans, who constructed the large *palaestra*, a vast, multi-purpose campus, which was at once a training area, a place for walking, a parade ground for the barracks, a slave market, and a cockfighting arena. The huge rectangular area—463 by 351 feet, or more than 160,000 square feet—was bounded by a wall as solid as the defenses of a *castrum*; on the inside, three raised porticoes surrounded the courtyard, in the center of which there was a swimming pool. The perfectly straight rows of plane trees planted here provide a striking example of the kind of arboreal architecture

On the table lies a purse full of money that will go to the owner of the winning cockerel. Before the fight, spectators placed bets in an atmosphere of feverish excitement.

that has been found in other gardens of the city.

Amateurs came here to throw the discus, to practice the long jump with weights in their hands, or to wrestle. Certain types of sport had a more military flavor: running in full armor, parading on horseback while skillfully executing the complicated maneuvers of the *ludus Troiae*, or Trojan game. In this way young men prepared themselves mentally and physically for their future role in city life.

After Physical Exercise, Baths Were Essential for the Hygiene of Young and Old Alike

The importance of the baths can be gauged from their number—three for the city of Pompeii alone— and from their location in the busiest and most accessible areas of the city: the Stabian Baths at the Holconius crossroads, the Forum Baths at the junction of the Via del Foro and the Via di Nola, and the Central Baths at the crossing of the *decumanus maximus* and the *cardo maximus*. These three establishments allow us to follow the development of bath architecture from the Samnite period, through the city's early days as a Roman colony, when the Forum Baths were constructed, right up to the time of the eruption, when the Central Baths were still unfinished.

The central block in all cases comprised the hot bath (*caldarium*), the warm steamroom (*tepidarium*), and the cold bath (*frigidarium*), arranged along a single east–west axis. It opened onto the *palaestra* courtyard, which had a

The *tepidarium* of the Forum Baths (far left) was heated by a large bronze brazier ornamented with calves' heads, the symbol of the donor, Nigidius Vaccula. The walls have niches set into them, which are divided by atlantes supporting an elaborate cornice carved with acanthus scrolls. The ceiling is decorated with stucco panels.

Light enters through a round window over the washbasin in the *caldarium* (left), in accordance with the recommendations of the Roman architect Vitruvius, while a rectangular opening illuminates the rest of the room.

Forum Baths

THE MEN'S BATH
I *Apodyterium* (changing room)
II *Frigidarium*
III *Tepidarium*
IV *Caldarium*
THE WOMEN'S BATH
1 *Apodyterium*
2 *Frigidarium*
3 *Tepidarium*
4 *Caldarium*

portico running around three sides, the fourth being taken up by an ornamental pool and the service quarters. In the Stabian Baths, the inclusion of a women's bath, separated from that of the men, meant that a sundial had to be used to regulate the opening times for men and women. The same separation of men and women can be found at the Forum Baths. The *frigidarium* was a circular, vaulted room; the entrance hall and dressing room, or *apodyterium*, were also vaulted, their ceilings covered with panels decorated with stucco.

A large staff were responsible for seeing to customers' needs. Some helped the disabled to climb the steps of the baths or to lower themselves into the cold pool; others helped to shower those who were not allowed to bathe. After the bath it was the turn of the hair-removers, perfumers, and masseurs (who were mainly black). These moments of relaxation were all part of the delights of living in Pompeii, and with the construction of the Central Baths, more and more Pompeians could devote themselves to bathing. In the bathing establishment of M. Crassus Frugi, there were even saltwater baths, though these were reserved for a privileged clientele.

Pompeians Had a Choice of Entertainment: Theater, Odeon, or Amphitheater

The theater, which dates from the Samnite period, c. 200 B.C., is both the oldest and the largest of the places of entertainment. In its horseshoe-shaped *cavea*, or auditorium, four semicircular walls support the great bank of earth which is covered by tiers of stone seats capable of holding five thousand spectators. To the south of the theater lay a garden

I n the *caldarium* of the Forum Baths (below), where the golden yellow walls are decorated with elegant red porphyry pilasters, visitors to the establishment passed from the hot bath to the *labrum*, a marble bowl from which sprang a jet of cold water. This *caldarium* is also shown in the 19th-century engraving (below right). The same engraver recorded the *tepidarium* of the Forum Baths (above right), with its elaborate stucco decoration.

Like many of his contemporaries, in 1853 the French painter Théodore Chassériau bowed to the fashion for the antique with this work entitled *Tepidarium: The Room Where the Women of Pompeii Came to Relax and Dry Themselves after Bathing*. However, the women are actually shown in the *tepidarium* of the men's bath at the Forum Baths! Apart from this anomaly, the painter was careful to reproduce the archaeological details with considerable accuracy. He quite correctly introduced into the scene the *tepidarium*'s bronze brazier and seats decorated with calves' heads (see p. 96). The painting evokes the same atmosphere of languid sensuality as the more famous *Turkish Bath* by Ingres and Delacroix' *Women of Algiers*.

Backstage, actors are busy choosing their masks and costumes.

From their position on the terraced seats of the *cavea*, the spectators had a perfect view down onto the stage. The stage shown below dates from the reconstruction of the large theater carried out under Nero, between 63 and 68. It was dominated by a richly decorated stage wall, with a vast, semicircular niche in the center, flanked on each side by a rectangular niche.

surrounded by an Ionic colonnade, where pleasant walks could be enjoyed during the intermissions. This vast open space was linked to the Via Stabiana and, by a wide flight of steps, to the Triangular Forum.

Between 63 and 68, a Roman-style *scenae frons* was built. Composed of a large, semicircular central niche flanked by two rectangular recesses, it had three openings cut into it: the royal entrance and two other doorways which were conventionally supposed to lead, on one side, to the city, and on the other, to the countryside. Behind the stage was a trench designed to hold the curtain that was lowered at the beginning of each performance; contrary to modern theatrical convention, the raising of the curtain signified the end of the show.

A second cultural venue, the Odeon, was built under Sulla. This indoor theater was intended for musical performances, poetry recitals, and lectures. The roofing of this structure, necessary for acoustical reasons, must have represented a considerable technical challenge; this explains why the *cavea*, which forms a perfect circle, seems very steep in comparison to the large theater. The thirty-nine tiers of seats made of tufa comfortably accommodated 1300 spectators, who could move around the theater with ease.

In the Odeon, elegant decorative details help to alleviate the plainness of the materials and the severe lines of the architecture. Tufa atlantes support each end of the back wall of the *cavea*, and griffins' claws are carved on the wall separating the *ima cavea* from the *media cavea*.

Twenty Thousand Spectators Went to Watch the Games at the Amphitheater

The amphitheater, which dates from the same period as the Odeon (c. 75 to 70 B.C.), was built in the form of an ellipse, backing onto a stretch of the city wall. Thirty-five rows of seats provided space for twenty thousand spectators, who took their places according to a strict social hierarchy, the most important citizens occupying the rows in the front and the lower classes

1

3

4

2

I

The Theater Quarter: Longitudinal Section

"On my first visit to Pompeii in 1857, I was struck by the beauty of the city's ruins....In addition to its great charm and novelty, the quarter around the theaters and the Triangular Forum offered me a series of buildings and monuments, almost all of which had preserved clear indications of their original decoration. The quarter includes a public square, known as the Triangular Forum, in the middle of which can still be found traces of a Greek temple...; a large and a small theater, quarters for soldiers, a public market, a temple dedicated to Isis...; private houses, a city gate, and the ramparts complete the ensemble."
—Paul-Emile Bonnet

These drawings by Paul-Emile Bonnet reflect the actual condition of the theater quarter in 1859 and his suggested reconstruction of it.

1 The gladiators' barracks
2 A side view of the stage wall, showing the means of access to it
3 The *parados,* or entrance for the chorus
4 The *cavea*
5 The Samnite *palaestra*

5

3 4

2

The Theater Quarter: Cross-Section from East to West

"These various buildings stand on land that slopes gently toward the sea; the way in which they cluster together, rising one above and behind the other, must have created some very picturesque views in this area of the city."

Paul-Emile Bonnet

This time the architect constructs his two perspective views from the south; in the reconstruction the outer wall is visible, together with two towers and the Stabian Gate. In both, the following buildings can be identified:

1 The Triangular Forum with the Doric temple, in front of which stands a beautiful *monopteros* surrounding a sacred well
2 The large theater
3 The Odeon
4 The Stabian Gate

Left: A plan of the theater quarter in its restored state.

Overleaf: A section of the large theater (detail from the reconstruction in the gatefold). This view clearly demonstrates the division of the *ima cavea*, the *media cavea*, and the *summa cavea*, which were placed one above the other.

relegated to the back, with poorer views. A whole society assembled here to acclaim the heroes of the games.

The organization of the games was in the hands of rich Pompeians, such as Cn. Alleius Nigidius Maius, who was proclaimed "prince of the impresarios." The aim was to get the highest number of pairs of gladiators to fight: perhaps as many as thirty in five days, or forty in four days. The calendar was packed in the prelude to the hot summer months; games were held on 4, 8, 9, 10, 11, 12, and 20 April, and on 2, 12, 13, 14, 16, and 31 May.

Games were also held in neighboring towns such as Nola, Nocera, and Pozzuoli in connection with regular feast days, such as the Games of Apollo (6–13 July), or to commemorate special events, like the consecration of the Temple of Vespasian or the opening of the Archives.

This enthusiasm for the games increased still further under the empire, and after 62 the quadriporticus of the large theater was converted into a barracks for the gladiators; individual cell rooms were constructed on two floors, while the courtyard was used for daily exercise.

Plan of the Amphitheater

I North axial gallery
II South axial gallery
III Gallery along the lesser axis
IV Corridors leading to the inner walkways
V Outer staircases
VI *Carceres* (rooms for the gladiators and animal cages)

To reduce the amount of earthmoving involved in the construction of the amphitheater, the architects arranged the ellipse so that it would back onto a portion of the city wall. The building measures 460 x 344 feet, and it encloses an arena 219 x 116 feet.

The gladiators tended to be professionals who had been taught combat techniques at specialized schools, and the impresarios were happy to pay large sums of money for their services. They were extraordinarily popular, no doubt because of a certain morbid fascination with men whose job it was to confront death every day—even though the public and magistrates often chose to spare the best gladiators, who were trained at the Capuan schools.

Gladiators were also celebrated for their amorous exploits. The eruption of 79 surprised one wealthy, bejeweled Pompeian lady in a cell at the barracks, who was found lying dead beside her gladiator lover.

Gladiatorial combat was not the only spectacle to be seen at the amphitheater. Other duels were held there: *venatio*—or

From either side of the amphitheater on the main north-south axis, two corridors lead into the arena—though one is bent at a right angle because of the city wall. A third corridor was probably used to remove dead animals and men. The spectators reached their seats either by the two corridors giving access to the internal walkways, or by the outer staircases which led to the upper levels.

This ivory sculpture of a heavily armed gladiator of the *hoplomachus* type (left), with his helmet, greaves, and dagger, suggests efficiency in combat.

"At about the same time [in 59], a trifling incident between the colonies of Nuceria [Nocera] and Pompeii provoked a terrible massacre; it arose at a gladiatorial show arranged by Livineius Regulus. During an exchange of taunts—characteristic of these disorderly country towns—abuse led to stone throwing, and then swords were drawn. The people of Pompeii, where the display was being held, came off best. Many Nucerians were taken home wounded and mutilated; many bereavements, too, were suffered by parents and children. The emperor instructed the Senate to investigate the affair, and the Senate passed it to the consuls. When they reported back, the Senate debarred Pompeii from holding any similar gathering for ten years ….Livineius and others held responsible for the disorders were exiled."

Tacitus
Annals, XIV, 17

fighting between men and lions, between wild and domesticated animals, or between lions and gazelles—often constituted the second half of the games. Although they glorified cruelty and indulged a taste for blood, these duels also demonstrated the courage of the combatants in their struggles with the ferocious wild beasts.

The Theater: A More Refined Form of Entertainment

Although Pompeians derived much pleasure from both pure comedy and pure tragedy, they did not object to

The paintings around the podium of the amphitheater enable us to follow the preparations for combat made by the various types of gladiator, from those on horseback (top left) to the *retiarii*, who fought with a net and trident. The center painting serves as a reminder that the amphitheater was also a hunting ground, where men fought bulls or wild boar, and where dogs fought boar, stags, and deer.

Scenes of gladiatorial combat engraved on the handle of this bronze strigil used in the baths (below) indicate the important role played by the games in the leisure time of Pompeians.

being moved from laughter to tears within the same performance. They loved the pathos and rhetoric, lyricism and violence of plays by the tragic poet Seneca, but they enjoyed still more comedies of manners based on works by Menander.

These held up a mirror to contemporary society, reflecting the everyday lives of the rich bourgeoisie, in which slaves and freedmen played an increasingly important role. In the house that is named after him, Menander is shown seated, crowned with a laurel wreath and holding a scroll of papyrus on which is written: "Menander was the first to write a New Comedy in four acts."

Especially popular with the public were farces that caricatured all kinds of familiar professions. Coal merchants, fortune-tellers, painters, and potters: anyone could become the target of the comic writer.

There was also a great vogue for other new forms of

entertainment: mime, in which the burlesque plots often revolved around adultery, and pantomime, those silent productions based purely on dance and gesture.

At the Odeon the Performances Were Somewhat More Sophisticated

Only the Odeon held itself aloof from this move toward popular taste; the select few went there to applaud the latest fashionable poet, who, wearing a laurel crown and a mask, would declaim his most recent verses. With this exception, the shows put on in the theaters were on the same level as the spectacles of the amphitheater.

Followed by a poor dwarf, a woman accompanies on her flute the dance of two men, one of whom plays the cymbals, while the other beats a tambourine. This mosaic illustrates a scene from a play by Menander.

Other forms of higher cultural entertainment appear to have been restricted to schools and the esoteric studies pursued by a mere handful of learned individuals in the privacy of their well-stocked libraries. Members of the lower classes, on the other hand, tended to demand light-hearted drama, broad farce that could make them roar with laughter, or bloody games that would simulta-neously excite and satisfy their instinct for violence.

A slave insults a young couple by making the sign of horns—the Neapolitan gesture *par excellence.* The man is trying to protect the young woman, who seems terrified. The slave's cloak is decorated with a fringe—a sign of wealth—and he may therefore represent one of Menander's heroes, a freedman named Pappos. His adventures provoked much amusement.

A t home or in the street, in private or in public, Pompeians were always in the presence of the gods. They worshiped them at regular hours in the many shrines and temples of the city, but they also devoted a good deal of their time to them when in the intimacy of their own homes.

CHAPTER VI
OF GODS AND MEN

Pompeii "the devout" made sacrifices day and night to its own native gods, as well as to exotic foreign deities. Bacchus (left) was worshiped everywhere. The Egyptian goddess Isis received praises from her faithful followers during the ceremony of the lustral waters (opposite), held daily at half past two in the afternoon.

The Most Important Cult: the Triad of Hercules, Bacchus, and Venus, Protectors of the Vine

These three divinities were often allowed a place in the *lararium*, the shrine at which the head of the household would daily worship his ancestors, or *lares*, surrounded by the members of his family and his slaves.

The *lararia* tended to feature paintings of Hercules, the legendary founder of Pompeii, while in small domestic shrines and courtyard gardens, Dionysiac

Venus Pompeiana, draped in blue and wearing a golden crown, stands in a chariot drawn by elephants, holding an olive branch. She represents triumphant Fortuna, who well deserves the palm and crown offered to her by two small cupids.

statuettes, theatrical masks, and busts of Bacchus glorified the god of wine. Pompeians also rendered homage to Venus, whom they addressed as Venus Pompeiana; as the city's official goddess, she was expected to bring them good luck and prosperity. Closely associated with Bacchus, she was an agrarian deity whose cult would later be combined with that of Ceres. She occupied a place of honor in the *lararia* and reigned over a large sanctuary close to the forum.

Two figures stand on either side of Venus' chariot: on the left is Fortuna, mistress of the world, bearing a cornucopia; on the right, the public Genius of Pompeii holds out a *patera*, or ceremonial dish.

Jupiter, Juno, Minerva: Worship of the Capitoline Triad Symbolized Support for Roman Sovereignty

These three deities enjoyed great popularity from the time of Sulla's founding of Pompeii. The Temple of Capitoline Jupiter dominates the forum; in the *cella*, the house of the god, a triple pedestal was designed to hold the three divine statues. Priests administered the official cult, but Jupiter, Juno, and Minerva were also worshiped in private houses.

The Temple of the Capitoline Triad, where Jupiter, Juno, and Minerva were worshiped, has a facade of six columns, each 28 feet high, supporting an impressive pediment. To the right of the temple stands the Arch of Tiberius.

The priests and priestesses of Isis wore white linen robes, shoes made of palm leaves or papyrus, and a headband decorated with the uraeus, or cobra. The priest (left) carries a bowl filled with lustral water, which he sprinkles about with an aspergillum. The priestess presents him with an *oenochoe*, or wine flask. The priest below is shaking a sistrum, or rattle, a form of musical instrument.

Isis, the Foreign Goddess

Roman religion had always proved very tolerant of foreign deities; through their trade links with the Sicilian ports and with Delos in the Cyclades the Pompeians discovered the Egyptian gods and introduced their worship into Campania. Their cult was particularly popular among the lower classes, the slaves, and families of freedmen who made up the staff of the great houses. Even after they had been freed, the descendants of freedmen continued to display their devotion to these gods, a devotion that the aristocracy later came to share.

The cult gradually took hold among the upper classes of the Pompeian population, eventually becoming the city's semi-official religion. The son of a freedman restored the Temple of Isis after its complete destruction by the earthquake of 62. Who was the generous patron? None other than a six-year-old child, N. Popidius Celsinus—assisted, admittedly, by his father. It was a gesture that opened the doors of the municipal council to him; but it is still proof of the enthusiasm for Isis felt by the city's aristocratic classes. At the houses of Loreius Tiburtinus and Julia Felix the garden contains a shrine dedicated to Isis, statuettes of pharaohs and Egyptian deities; important citizens like Cn. Poppaeus Habitus worshiped the goddess with great fervor.

In the Temple of Isis daily ceremonies were performed in her name. Before sunrise, the image of the goddess was presented to her adoring followers, who gathered in front of the temple to thank her in their prayers and to shake the *sistrum* in her honor. The worshipers would remain seated, deep in prayer and contemplation, until after sunrise; the service ended with an invocation to the newly risen sun. At two o'clock in the afternoon a second ceremony was held for the adoration of consecrated water.

In addition to these daily rites, Isis was the focus for elaborate festivities, the most important of which was the *navigium Isidis*, celebrated on 5 March; as the patron of sailors, it was appropriate that she should be honored at a time of year when they were beginning to set sail once more, after the winter. The second festival, Isia (13–16 November), commemorated Isis' discovery of the body of Osiris. Public joy was translated into secret initiation rites undergone by the servants of Isis, who renounced their past life and, through this rebirth, committed themselves to leading a purer life in the future.

A traveler, recognizable by his short tunic and long staff, asks the sybil to provide him with a philter. It is natural that, as a stranger to the place, he should seek magical assistance before entering the city.

The Villa of the Mysteries: Scenes from the Myth of Dionysos

In the Villa of the Mysteries, a suburban mansion not far from Pompeii, an elaborate fresco decorates a room discreetly hidden at the center of the house. It is dedicated to Dionysos, the universally beneficent god. Twenty-nine figures and numerous scenes can be made out running continuously around the room. The main protagonists are Dionysos himself—indicated by his *thyrsus,* a staff entwined with vine leaves and ivy—and Semele, his mother; they can be seen embracing in the center of the lower panel (left). On either side of this central image, two myths unfold: that of Dionysos and that of Semele, each of which is mirrored by the life of a priestess.

The Villa of the Mysteries: Scenes from the Myth of Semele

The woman at her toilet (above) symbolizes Semele preparing for her marriage to Zeus. The portion of the fresco shown opposite develops the allegory of Semele's pregnancy and the birth of Dionysos. For a fuller interpretation of these scenes, see pp. 186–91.

Not all Pompeians were so spiritually elevated, however, and some went to any lengths to ward off the evil eye—magic urns, ghostly hands. This distinctive brand of religious sensibility derived from Bacchic rites. In the 70s of the 1st century the new Christian religion had yet to reach the people of Pompeii.

Pompeians Recognized Only One God on Earth: the Emperor

The imperial cult transcended all other cults, and all divine qualities were attributed to the emperor. As a descendant of Venus, the lover of Mars, and mother of Romulus, the emperor inevitably drew all the divine triads into his own orbit. Thus, the college of slaves and freedmen who honored Mercury and Maia, the *ministri Mercuri et Maiae*, became known between 14 and 2 B.C. as the *ministri augusti Mercuri et Maiae*, and after 2 B.C. simply as that of the *ministri augusti*.

In the center of the courtyard of the Temple of Vespasian, a white marble altar bears a scene associated with the imperial cult. The priest, his head covered by a fold of his toga, pours a libation; he may represent the Emperor Vespasian himself, in his role as the supreme pontiff. Two *lictores*, a flute player, and two young boys bring the sacred implements, while the sacrificial bull is led to the altar by the executioner and his assistant.

By associating himself with all things divine, the emperor offered every citizen the opportunity to worship him, regardless of ethnic or social differences. The freedmen, who played an important role in economic life, formed the college of *augustales*. They took on responsibility for the street shrines to the *lares* of the Crossroads, the *lares compitales*, later known as the Augustan *lares*, organizing the same ceremonies as the *vicomagistri* (area magistrates) in Rome.

An elaborate hierarchy composed of priests and priestesses, *augustales*, and *ministri* pledged themselves to the emperor. The forum celebrates this imperial glory through its statues and triumphal arches. The fact that space was set aside for the imperial cult can come as a surprise in certain contexts: there is a chapel in the market (*macellum*); in the Temple of the Lares; the Temple of Vespasian; the building of Eumachia; even in the large *palaestra*, where each young man had to perform propitiatory rites before exercising. This syncretism is most clearly expressed in the Temple of Apollo, where the cult was directed toward Apollo and Diana, to Mercury and Maia, and, inevitably, to the emperor. Gradually, the triads lost favor and were replaced by the imperial monad.

Private Religion

Pompeians devoted a fairly substantial portion of their free time to religious observance in their own homes, where, as in the Villa of the Mysteries, the decoration sometimes evokes a higher world that only the initiated are permitted to enter. The vitality of private religion is clear from the care with which the *lararia* in certain houses were restored and embellished after the earthquake of 62. Pompeii was a pious city, but not a bigoted one, in which each individual was free to express his or her own spiritual preferences through respect for the imperial religion, which pervaded all that was sacred.

Like the houses, the streets in Pompeii belonged to the gods; the *lares* were often depicted on the surface of the walls. This shrine in the House of the Vettii takes the form of a classical temple facade, with a pediment supported by two columns.

On the rear wall, a Genius dressed in a toga is flanked by two *lares*, who have the appearance of young men; wearing short, loose tunics, they raise high their drinking horns. At the bottom of the *lararium*, a great, many-coiled serpent with a crested head symbolizes the male ancestor, protector of the household, whom these libations are intended to placate.

Though they were blessed by the goddess of love, Pompeians did not worship Venus alone; nor did they lead carefree lives entirely free of the fear of death. The cemeteries just outside the city gates were an ever-present reminder of mortality, of the law that applies to all, blindly striking young and old alike.

CHAPTER VII
LOVE AND DEATH IN POMPEII

Even in the happiest moments of life, Pompeians were never entirely liberated from thoughts of death. No one was more aware than they of how short was the time for living, loving, and dying.

No other city in the Roman world has played the part of love's messenger better than Pompeii. Venus, in all her many guises, ruled supreme there. Alongside the Venus Pompeiana, we find the Venus Marina, or Venus of the Shell, carelessly revealing her exquisite naked form. Elsewhere, she appears in a more discreetly erotic context, in an allegory of the love of Mars and Venus.

Meanwhile, the earthly Venus manifested her power in the quarters of ill repute, in the lupanars and dark corners. Graffiti covering the facades of houses, shops, and public buildings reveal a people who talked openly of love. We find crude remarks about amorous prowess, the names and nicknames of pimps and procuresses, prostitutes (both boys and girls), and colorful illustrations in the half-light of cells depicting the techniques of experienced whores. Elsewhere, an obscene Priapus or a scene of bestial coupling can be found side by side with idyllic images of romantic love: Hylas assailed by the nymphs, Narcissus at the fountain, Hero and Leander…. In the *triclinium* of the House of the Vettii, for example, panels depict pairs of mythical and legendary lovers: Perseus and Andromeda, Apollo and Daphne, Dionysos and Ariadne.

Pompeians could produce a charming, discreetly allusive poem to match any occasion, no matter how

Inspired by the nearby sea, Pompeians honored the *Venus Marina* (above), whose shell is drawn along by cupids, while a favorable breeze swells the veil above her head.

In Pompeii it is hard to avoid the clichéd image of the loves of Mars and Venus. Sometimes the two deities provocatively display their naked forms, but more often they are shown correctly dressed, rather like a bourgeois couple. Here, Mars, in military dress, has not yet removed his helmet, lance, and breastplate, while Venus is swathed in a long tunic covered by a light cloak. The hand of Mars, straying over Venus' breast, is the only clue to the amorous significance of the scene.

Pompeians were very fond of erotic images, depicting either the loves of the gods or Priapic prowess. The sight of the figure (far left) weighing a huge phallus never fails to arouse the interest of visitors to the House of the Vettii. Placed in the entrance hall, the scene was designed to avert evil, the idea being that such a sight would disarm the antique visitor, thus cleansing him of any evil designs he might have had.

Two lovers recline on a bed, sharing a meal (left). The man drinks wine from a glass drinking horn, while his lover, her nudity veiled by a diaphanous garment as delicate as a spider's web, keeps a watchful eye on the effect that the wine is having on her partner. Nevertheless, the scene remains only discreetly erotic.

improper. The lover hurrying to meet the object of his affections rails against the delay imposed by the mule-driver's thirst: "If you were the one suffering the fires of love, muleteer, you would be in more of a hurry to see Venus. I love a young and handsome boy; I beg you, spur on your mules…. You've finished your drink, let's go; take up the reins and shake them. Take me to Pompeii where my sweet love is waiting."

Elsewhere, Venus is invoked to further a man's pursuit of love: "Do not forget me, dear mistress, I beg you, by Venus Fisica!" The goddess is also called upon to assist the lover in wreaking mortal vengeance: "I beg you, let my rival perish!" But the disappointed lover, cruelly defeated, turns on the goddess, threatening to tear her limb from limb and to return her false-hearted treachery blow for blow.

In general, however, the Pompeian lover is calm and gentle, claiming only the right to love: "Lovers are like bees; their lives are sweet as honey." The art of love is in some respects an art of living: "Long live lovers! Death to those who know not how to love! Double death to those who hinder love!"

Pompeian Women Were Not Just Objects of Fleeting Desire, but Precious, Lifelong Companions

Ever since the age of Nero, a disillusioned society, infected with world-weariness, had been searching for something to give life new meaning; in the virtues of the Pompeian wife it found a fresh ideal. The torments of Ixion and of Dirce, for example, stressed the value of self-discipline and submission to the will of the gods. In the House of the Vettii (VI, 15), the mural painters contrasted the legitimate love of Peleus and Thetis with more unhappy, illicit affairs, and offered divine couples as a model for earthly lovers. Their unions, untainted by lechery or corruption, represent the fusion of sensuality and morality.

By contrast, this painting from the rear kitchen of the House of the Vettii, a scene of amorous dalliance with a servant, takes sexual realism quite far. The master of the house is exercising his "rights" over a young servant, in a room whose plain decorations contrast sharply with the sumptuous cushions and covers of the room opposite.

Faced with this Venus (left), who emphasizes her natural charms with golden netting, a young Priapus betrays his excitement.

The Street of the Sepulchers, by J. P. Hackert.

"It's a big mistake to have nice houses just for when you're alive and not worry about the one you have to live in for much longer."
Petronius, *Satiricon*

Love Inspires Feelings of Piety, Reverence for Gods, and Respect for People, Whether Living or Dead

The roads leading to Pompeii, lined with ostentatious tombs, are like so many streets of the dead; and yet the image of death is not a distressing one. Among the tombs and the cypress trees that shade them, the shadow of death has no chill. The orchards in these cemeteries are in flower, and in the sunshine inscriptions and relief carvings glorify the names of magistrates and other citizens. Shops, inns, and sumptuous country mansions stand among the tombs; life continues alongside death. Apart, perhaps, from the occasional funeral ceremony, a moving tribute paid to the dead by relatives and friends, and the sobs of a mourning family breaking the stillness, nothing would have suggested sorrow in these streets.

The history of the city can be read in the inscriptions on the tombs; the burial grounds are the repository of past glories.

In the cemeteries we rediscover the social hierarchy of the living, as the aristocratic classes perpetuated the memory of their high offices and occupations. But these important citizens did not lie alone within their lofty tombs; the small niches in the burial vault held the bones of their relatives, while within the sepulchral wall were the more humble members of the household, whom they had fed and nurtured. An amphora or small urn was sufficient to hold the cremated remains of a slave or freedman; a stone was laid over the mouth of the buried amphora and pierced by a tube, through which libations could be poured. A stela, sometimes of marble, recorded the servant's name, and in the case of one of Livy's slaves, the marble was carved in the shape of a face, framed by braided hair. Peace reigned among the dead as it did among the living, and even in a society founded on slavery, death abolished class divisions.

The architecture of the funerary monuments is extremely varied, and many are striking for their majestic character. In the necropolis by the Herculaneum Gate stands the Tomb of the Istacidii, a circular temple surrounded by half-columns; the *tholos,* or vaulted chamber, composed of Ionic columns, shelters statues of members of the family.

The Tomb of Umbricius Scaurus, a wealthy manufacturer and dealer in *garum*, exhibits a decorative scheme inspired by the games held at the amphitheater, showing gladiators and animals of the hunt.

The necropolis at the Nucerian Gate contains several monuments raised by women to the glory of their husbands: Veia Barchilla on behalf of Agrestinus Equitius Pulcher, or Eumachia's grandiose apse. Another interesting tomb is that constructed for her husband by Naevoleia Tyche, which carries a bas-relief showing a ship entering the harbor.

A Catastrophic Eruption Brings the Death of Pompeii Itself

The proud sepulchers and luxurious tombs cannot erase the memory of those who died in the summer of 79, who had as their shroud a layer of ash and pumice many feet thick.

Nothing could be more poignant than the dead discovered in 1961 close to the Nucerian Gate. Three families had clustered together under a roof to shelter from the hail of burning stones; they had died while trying to escape. One woman had fallen to her knees, pressing a cloth to her mouth to protect herself from the deadly fumes. Her husband must have watched her die, still holding the hand of their child, before finally succumbing himself.

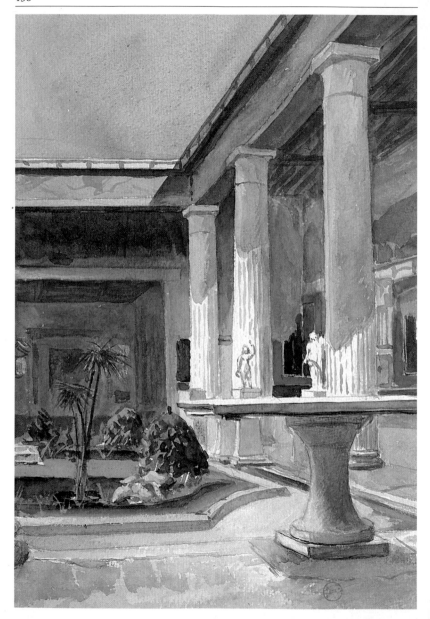

DOCUMENTS

The history of Pompeii, its destruction, and its
resurrection in the words of those who visited the city
and fell in love with it, who understood its value, and
who did their best to preserve it for others.

The Campanian Earthquake

The Roman philosopher Seneca, who was Nero's minister, is best known for his Dialogues, *in which he discusses our knowledge of the workings of the human soul. Toward the end of his life he also became interested in the natural world. His* Natural Questions *were intended as a scientific encyclopedia covering all natural phenomena. The earthquake of 62, which destroyed several monuments in Pompeii, is described in this work.*

Pompeii, the famous city in Campania, has been laid low by an earthquake which also disturbed all the adjacent districts. The city is in a pleasant bay, some distance from the open sea, and bounded by the shores of Surrentum and Stabiae on one side and of Herculaneum on the other; the shores meet there.

In fact, it occurred in days of winter, a season which our ancestors used to claim was free from such disaster. This earthquake was on the Nones [5] of February, in the consulship of Regulus and Verginius. It caused great destruction in Campania, which had never been safe from this danger but had never been damaged, and time and again had got off with a fright. Also, part of the town of Herculaneum is in ruins, and even the structures which are left standing are shaky. The colony of Nuceria escaped destruction but still has much to complain about. Naples also lost many private dwellings but no public buildings, and was only mildly grazed by the great disaster; but some villas collapsed, others here

Bas-relief showing the effects of the 62 earthquake on the various monuments of Pompeii. The Temple of the Capitoline Triad is clearly visible.

proposed work, and the concurrence of the disaster at this time, requires that we discuss the causes of these earthquakes.

It is necessary to find solace for distressed people and to remove their great fear. Yet can anything seem adequately safe to anyone if the world itself is shaken, and its most solid parts collapse? Where will our fears finally be at rest if the one thing which is immovable in the universe and fixed, so as to support everything that leans upon it, starts to waver; if the earth loses the characteristic it has: stability?

What hiding-place will creatures find, where will they flee in their anxiety, if fear arises from below and is drawn from the depths of the earth? There is panic on the part of all when buildings creak and give signs of falling. Then everybody hurls himself headlong outside, abandons his household possessions, and trusts to his luck in the outdoors.

What hiding-place do we look to, what help, if the earth itself is causing the ruin, if what protects us, upholds us, on which cities are built, which some speak of as a kind of foundation of the universe, separates and reels?

Seneca
Quaestiones Naturales, VI

and there shook without damage. To these calamities others were added: they say that a flock of hundreds of sheep was killed, statues were cracked, and some people were so shocked that they wandered about as if deprived of their wits. The thread of my

Pompeii, 24 August 79

Pliny the Younger was the nephew of Pliny the Elder, admiral of the Mediterranean fleet based at Misenum. The uncle was a man of encyclopedic knowledge, who left thirty-seven books of a Natural History. *In 104 Pliny the Younger, who was a talented letter writer, wrote two letters (VI, 16 and 20) to the historian Tacitus (c. 55–120), in which he described the death of his uncle on the coast near Stabiae and his emotions at the time. His feelings must have been similar to those experienced by the men and women of Pompeii.*

PLINE LE JEUNE.

Landon direx.ᵗ

My uncle was stationed at Misenum in active command of the fleet. The ninth day before the Calends of September [24 August], in the early afternoon, my mother drew to his attention a cloud of unusual size and appearance. He had been out in the sun, had taken a cold bath, eaten a light lunch while lying down, and was then working at his books. He called for his shoes and climbed up to a place that would give him the best view of the phenomenon. It was not clear at that distance from which mountain the cloud was rising (it was afterward known to be Vesuvius). Its general appearance can best be expressed as being like an umbrella pine, for it rose to a great height on a sort of trunk and then split off into branches, I imagine because it was thrust upward by the first blast and then left unsupported as the pressure subsided, or else it was borne down by its own weight so that it spread out and gradually dispersed. In places it looked white, elsewhere blotched and dirty, according to the amount of soil and ashes it carried with it. My uncle's scholarly acumen saw at once that it was important enough for a closer inspection, and he ordered a boat to be made ready, telling me I could come with him if I wished. I replied that I preferred to go on with my studies, and as it happened he had himself given me some writing to do.

As he was leaving the house he was handed a message from Rectina, wife of Cascus, whose house was at the foot of the mountain, so that escape was impossible except by boat. She was terrified by the danger threatening her and implored him to rescue her from her fate. He changed his plans, and what he had begun in a spirit of inquiry he completed as a hero. He gave orders for the warships to be launched and went on board himself with the intention of bringing help to many more people besides Rectina, for this lovely stretch of coast was thickly populated.

He hurried to the place which everyone else was hastily leaving, steering his course straight for the danger zone. He was entirely fearless, describing each new movement and phase of the portent to be noted down exactly as he observed them. Ashes were already falling, hotter and thicker as the ships drew near, followed by bits of pumice and blackened stones, charred and cracked by the flames: then suddenly they were in shallow water, and the shore was blocked by the debris

"Meanwhile, on Mount Vesuvius broad sheets of fire and leaping flames blazed at several points."

from the mountain. For a moment my uncle wondered whether to turn back, but when the helmsman advised this he refused, telling him that Fortune stood by the courageous and they must make for the home of Pomponianus at Stabiae. He was cut off there by the breadth of the bay (for the shore gradually curves around a basin filled by the sea) so that he was not as yet in danger, though it was clear that this would come nearer as it spread. Pomponianus had therefore already put his belongings on board ship, intending to escape if the contrary wind fell. The wind was of course full in my uncle's favor, and he was able to bring his ship in. He embraced his terrified friend, cheered and encouraged him, and thinking he could calm his fears by showing his own composure, gave orders that he was to be carried to the bathroom. After his bath he lay down and dined; he was quite cheerful, or at any rate he pretended he was, which was no less courageous.

Meanwhile on Mount Vesuvius broad sheets of fire and leaping flames blazed at several points, their bright glare emphasized by the darkness of night. My uncle tried to allay the fears of his companions by repeatedly declaring that these were nothing but bonfires left by the peasants in their terror, or else empty houses on fire in the districts they had abandoned.

Then he went to rest and certainly slept, for as he was a stout man his breathing was rather loud and heavy and could be heard by people coming

Nothing could stand up to the rain of ash. After the houses, the temples succumbed: here, the Temple of Isis, the Pompeians' favorite Egyptian goddess.

and going outside his door. By this time the courtyard giving access to his room was full of ashes mixed with pumice stones, so that its level had risen, and if he had stayed in the room any longer he would never have got out. He was wakened, came out, and joined Pomponianus and the rest of the household, who had stayed up all night. They debated whether to stay indoors or take their chance in the open, for the buildings were now shaking with violent shocks, and seemed to be swaying to and fro as if they were torn from their foundations. Outside, on the other hand, there was the danger of falling pumice stones, even though these were light and porous; after comparing the risks they chose the latter. In my uncle's case one reason outweighed the other, but for the others it was a choice of fears. As a protection against falling objects they put pillows on their heads tied down with cloths.

Elsewhere there was daylight by this time, but they were still in darkness, blacker and denser than any ordinary night, which they relieved by lighting torches and various kinds of lamps. My uncle decided to go down to the shore, to see at first hand whether it was possible to escape by sea; but they found the waves still wild and dangerous. There a sheet was spread on the ground for my uncle to lie down, and he called repeatedly for cold water, which he drank. Then the flames and smell of sulfur which heralded the approaching fire drove the others to take flight. Aroused, my uncle struggled to his feet, leaning on two slaves, but immediately collapsed. I assume that his breathing was impeded by the dense fumes, which blocked his windpipe—for it was constitutionally weak and

narrow, and often inflamed. When daylight returned—two days after the last time he had seen it—his body was found intact and uninjured, still fully clothed as in life. He looked more like a man sleeping than a dead man.

You tell me that the letter in which, at your request, I described the death of my uncle has made you want to know what fears and even what dangers I myself experienced, having been left behind at Misenum (in fact, I had reached this point when I interrupted

On 11 May 1771 Vesuvius reawoke. William Hamilton, the English ambassador, executed several watercolors of the subject.

myself). Although I tremble at the very memory, I will begin.

After my uncle's departure, I gave the rest of the day to study—the object which had kept me at home. Afterward I bathed, dined, and retired to short and broken sleep. For several days we had experienced earth shocks, which hardly alarmed us as they are frequent in Campania. But that night they became so violent that it seemed the world was not only being shaken, but turned upside down. My mother rushed to my bedroom—I was just rising, as I intended to wake her if she was asleep. We sat down in the courtyard of the house, which separated it by a short distance from the sea. Whether from courage or inexperience (I was eighteen at the time), I called for a volume of Titus Livius and began to read, and even continued my notations from it, as if nothing were the matter. At this moment a friend of my uncle's arrived; he had just returned from Spain to see him. When he saw me sitting there, with my mother, when he saw me reading, he criticized me for my passivity and lack of concern; I continued to pay just as much enthusiastic attention to my book.

Though it was the first hour of the day, the light appeared to us still faint and uncertain. And though we were in an open place, it was narrow, and the buildings around us were so unsettled that the collapse of walls seemed a certainty. We decided to get out of town to escape this menace. The panic-stricken crowds followed us, in response to that instinct of fear which causes people to follow where others lead. In a long close tide they harassed and jostled us. When we were clear of the houses, we stopped, as we

encountered fresh prodigies and terrors. Though our carts were on level ground, they were tossed about in every direction, and even when weighted with stones could not be kept steady. The sea appeared to have shrunk, as if withdrawn by the tremors of the earth. In any event, the shore had widened, and many sea creatures were beached on the sand. In the other direction loomed a horrible black cloud ripped by sudden bursts of fire, writhing snakelike and revealing sudden flashes larger than lightning.

Then my uncle's friend from Spain began to argue with great energy and urgency. "If your brother," he said, "if your uncle is alive, he would want you to be saved; if he has perished, he would have wanted you to survive. Why, then, do you delay your escape?" We replied that we could not think of our own safety before finding out what had happened to him. Without a moment's further delay, he left us abruptly and escaped the danger in a frantic headlong rush. Soon after, the cloud began to descend upon the earth and cover the sea. It had already surrounded and obscured Capreae [Capri], and blotted out Cape Misenum. My mother now began to beg, urge, and command me to escape as best I could. A young man could do it; she, burdened with age and corpulence, would die easy if only she had not caused my death. I replied that I would not be saved without her. Taking her hand, I hurried her along. She complied reluctantly, and not without self-reproach for hindering me.

And now came the ashes, but at first sparsely. I turned around. Behind us, an ominous thick smoke, spreading over the earth like a flood, followed us. "Let's go into the fields while we can still see the way," I told my mother—for I was afraid that we might be crushed by the mob on the road in the midst of the darkness. We had scarcely agreed when we were enveloped in night—not a moonless night or one dimmed by cloud, but the darkness of a sealed room without lights. To be heard were only the shrill cries of women, the wailing of children, the shouting of men. Some were calling to their parents, others to their children, others to their wives—knowing one another only by voice. Some wept for themselves, others for their relations. There were those who, in their very fear of death, invoked it. Many lifted up their hands to the gods, but a great number believed there were no gods, and that this was to be the world's last, eternal night. Some added to the real danger with false or illusory terrors: "In Misenum," they would say, "such and such a building has collapsed, and some

other is in flames." This might not be true, but it was believed.

A curious brightness revealed itself to us not as daylight but as approaching fire; but it stopped some distance from us. Once more, darkness and ashes, thick and heavy. From time to time we had to get up and shake them off for fear of being actually buried and crushed under their weight. I can boast that in so great a danger, I did not utter a single word or a single lamentation that could have been construed as weakness. I believed that one and all of us would perish—a wretched but strong consolation in my dying. But the darkness lightened, and then like smoke or cloud dissolved away. Finally a genuine daylight came; the sun shone, but pallidly, as in an eclipse. And then, before our terror-stricken gaze everything appeared changed—covered by a thick layer of ashes like an abundant snowfall.

We returned to Misenum, where we refreshed ourselves as best we could. We passed an anxious night between hope and fear—though chiefly the latter, for the earthquakes continued, and some pessimistic people were giving a ghoulish turn to their own and their neighbors' calamities by horrifying predictions. Even so, my mother and I—despite the danger we had experienced and the danger which still threatened—had no thought of leaving until we should receive some word of my uncle.

Such were the events; and you will read about them without the slightest intention of including the information in your works, as they are unworthy of history.... Adieu!

Pliny the Younger
Letters to Tacitus, VI, 16 and 20

A Pioneer in Pompeii

Johann Joachim Winckelmann was a self-taught enthusiast of classical art. Sent to Rome in 1757, he became a respected antiquities expert. In 1762 he discovered the excavations at Herculaneum and Pompeii, and criticized the lack of organization that existed there.

Joh. Winkelmann.

A well dug for the prince of Elbeuf, at a small distance from his house, was the first thing that gave occasion to the discovery they are now pursuing. The prince had built this house in order to make his constant residence in it. It lay behind the Franciscan convent, at the extremity of, and upon, a rock of lava near the sea. It afterward fell into the hands of the house of Falletti of Naples, from whom the present king of Spain purchased it, in order to make a fishing seat of it. The well in question had been sunk near the garden of the barefooted Carmelites. To form it, they were obliged to dig through the lava to the live rock, where the workmen found, under the ashes of Mount Vesuvius, three large clothed female statues. These the Austrian viceroy very justly laid claim to, and, keeping part of them in his hands, ordered them to Rome, where they were repaired. They were then presented to Prince Eugene, who placed them in his gardens, at Vienna....

On the discovery of these antiquities, orders were given to the prince of Elbeuf not to dig any further. Thirty years, however, were suffered to elapse, before any more notice was taken of them. At length, the present king of Spain, as soon as by the conquest of Naples he found himself in peaceable possession of it, chose Portici for his spring residence; and, as the well was still in being, ordered the works begun at the bottom of it to be continued, till they reached some buildings. This well still subsists. It runs down perpendicularly through the lava to the middle of the theater, (the first building discovered), which receives no light but by it. Here an inscription was found containing the name of Herculaneum, which, by giving room to guess what place they had hit upon, determined his majesty to proceed further.

The direction of this work was given to a Spanish engineer, called Roch Joachim Alcubierre, who had followed his majesty to Naples, and is now colonel, and chief of the body of engineers at Naples. This man, who (to use the Italian proverb), knew as much of antiquities, as the moon does of lobsters, has been, through his want of capacity, the occasion of many antiquities being lost. A single fact will be sufficient to prove it. The workmen having discovered a large public inscription (to what buildings it belonged, I can't say) in letters of brass two palms high; he ordered these letters to be torn from the wall, without first taking a copy of them, and thrown pell mell into a basket; and then presented them, in that condition, to the king. They were afterward exposed for many years in the cabinet, where every one

was at liberty to put them together as he pleased. Some imagined they made these two words, IMP. AUG. I shall presently relate how a brazen four-horse chariot was served, by the same engineer's directions.

Don Roch having in time attained a higher rank, the superintendence and conduct of the works in question were committed to a Swiss officer, called Charles Weber, now a major; and it is to his good sense, that we are indebted for all the good steps since taken, to bring to light this treasure of antiquities. The first thing he did was to make an exact map of all the subterranean galleries, and the buildings they led to. This map he rendered still more intelligible, by a minute historical account of the whole discovery. The ancient city is to be seen in it as if freed from all the rubbish, with which it is actually incumbered. The inside of the buildings, the most

The kings of Naples had a museum constructed close to their palace at Portici, and had the antique objects discovered at Herculaneum transported there for display with great solemnity.

private rooms, and the gardens, as well as the particular spots, where every thing taken out of them was found, appear in this map, just as they would, if they were laid quite bare. But nobody is permitted to see those drawings.

The happy issue of the works undertaken at Herculaneum proved a motive for opening the earth in other places; and the doing this soon enabled them to ascertain the situation of the ancient Stabia, and led them, at Pompeii, to the vast remains of an amphitheater, built on a hill, part of which, however, had always been visible above ground. The diggings in these places proved far less expensive than the diggings in Herculaneum, as there was no lava to dig through. The subterranean works at Pompeii are those which promise most, for here they are not only sure of proceeding step by step in a great city, but have

found out the principal street of it, which runs in a straight line. But, notwithstanding all this certainty of their being able to find treasures unknown to our ancestors, the works for that purpose are carried on in a very slow and indolent manner; there being but fifty men, including the Algerine and Tunisian slaves, employed in all these subterraneous places. Great a city as Pompeii is known to have been, I, in my last journey, found but eight men at work on the ruins of it.

To compensate for this neglect the method observed in digging is such that it is impossible the least spot should escape unnoticed. On both sides of one principal trench, carried on in a right line, the workmen alternately hollow out chambers, six palms in length, breadth, and height; removing the rubbish, as they proceed, from every one of these chambers, to the chamber opposite it, that was last hollowed out. This method is taken, not only with a view of lessening the expense, but of supporting the earth over one chamber, with the rubbish taken out of another.

I know that strangers, particularly travelers, who can take but a cursory view of these works, wish, that all the rubbish was entirely removed, so as to give them an opportunity of seeing, as in the plan of which I have been speaking, the inside of the whole subterranean city of Herculaneum. They are apt to impeach the taste of the Court, and of those who direct these works. But this is a mere prejudice, which a rational examination of the nature of the spot, and other circumstances, would soon conquer....

Those who have a mind to see the walls of ancient buildings formerly buried in the same manner, may satisfy their curiosity at Pompeii. But few persons, except Englishmen, have resolution enough to go so far.... At Pompeii the ground may be dug up, and turned topsy-turvy, without any risk, and at a small expense, the land lying over it being of little value. Formerly, indeed, it used to produce the most delicious wine; but that it now produces is so middling, that the country would suffer very little by the entire destruction of its vineyards....

It appears by the indolent manner in which these works are conducted, that a fine field of discovery must remain to posterity.... But the court is so well satisfied with the discoveries now making, that it has forbid the earth to be dug any where else below a certain depth.

Johann Joachim Winckelmann,
A Critical Account of the Situation and Destruction...of Herculaneum, Pompeii, and Stabia, 1771

Herculaneum: An Inventory

The Count de Caylus, archaeologist, writer, and engraver (1692–1765), was fascinated by Pompeii and Herculaneum. Like Winckelmann, he resented the secrecy with which the Neapolitan court surrounded the site. He translated Winckelmann's pamphlet into French and made it more widely known, thereby exacerbating the suspicion with which the sovereigns tended to regard foreigners.

All the works of art found in Herculaneum are displayed in the exhibition rooms that his majesty the king of Sicily had built at Portici. Those entrusted with the protection of this collection, loyal to the instructions of their prince, will not allow a single note to be taken there, and nothing can escape their vigilance. The only remedy, therefore, is to remember at leisure the most important things you noticed, neglecting those details which even the best memory can retain only at the expense of more significant elements. This you may judge for yourselves by my brief account of the entire collection of antiquities to be found in the museum at Portici.

About 700 fragments of paintings; 350 statues, including portrait busts of varying quality, made of either bronze or marble; 700 different vases of various shapes and sizes, almost all of bronze and the majority designed for everyday use; about 20 bronze tripods; around 40 candelabras or chandeliers of the same metal, which supported the lamps used to light the apartments; 800 manuscripts; and 600 other smaller items, such as lamps, instruments, rings, bracelets, necklaces, mirrors, etc.

I include in the number of statues mentioned earlier all the small bronze and marble figurines which are nowadays to be found in almost every collection of antiquities. Such works deserve our attention only when they display elegant forms, when they reveal the attributes used to characterize the gods of the ancients, or, finally, when they provide a true likeness of those famous men whose actions and writings we so admire. I will confine myself to the mention of some small busts that bear the names of Epicurus, Zeno,

Demosthenes, and of the Epicurean philosopher Hermachus. The number of life-size statues amounts to about forty, of which approximately half are in bronze and the rest marble....

It would seem that at the time of the eruption of Vesuvius which destroyed the town of Herculaneum, the inhabitants had sufficient time to escape the danger and to rescue most of their belongings; this explains why no items of gold jewelry and only small silver vases have been found. Vases made of bronze have been unearthed in large quantities, and in general they reveal excellent workmanship and attractive forms. The decoration on these takes a hundred different forms, but is always tasteful. In some cases there are foliage motifs, inlaid with silver, encircling the rim or neck of the vase; in others pretty little intertwining figures form the handles; most take the form of jugs, bowls, or saucers. Antique-dealers, who always try to

elaborate on the history of the items they are selling in order to increase the value of their labors, will usually tell you that such vessels were sacrificial vases; but the vast quantities that are found every day in Herculaneum prove that they were simply made for everyday use. Nevertheless, the care taken to embellish them also shows, at the same time, that Greek influence was not confined to larger works, but extended even to the smaller objects. There is one such class of objects in particular that I cannot pass by without a mention: it consists of the different types of scales, and especially those with two bronze feet, which are equivalent to about 11 inches of our imperial foot.

There is also a loaf that catches the attention of the curious; on it is an inscription, which would be difficult enough to read as it is, were one allowed to examine it without obstruction, and which is even more impossible to decipher since it has been

A Greek manuscript found in the Villa of the Papyri at Herculaneum.

covered with glass. The inscription consists of two lines, and I believe I could make out, in the second line, the Latin word for chick peas. It appears that the police ordered that every loaf be marked with the type of flour that had been used to make it.

As for the rest, all the different types of objects excavated in Herculaneum could provide material for several articles; but I only wish to deal here with the manuscripts, which seem to me the most significant finds. To get a clearer picture of these, you must imagine a fairly long strip of paper, about a foot wide. The whole length of this paper would have been covered with several columns of text, each separated from the next, and going from right to left. The sheet was then rolled up in such a way that as you opened the scroll, you had before you the first column or page of the work, the last one being at the center.

The manuscripts from Herculaneum were found in a room in a palatial could be hoped for using this method was to preserve a single page or column of a manuscript that might perhaps contain a hundred.

At this point a hard-working and patient monk introduced himself, and suggested a way of unrolling the manuscripts completely. He carried out experiments which took up a great deal of time, but which proved successful; and he has persisted with these experiments, at the same speed and with the same success. He looks for the outer edge of the manuscript and attaches to it several silk threads, which he rolls around some pins mounted on a small frame. He carefully turns these pins, and the manuscript unfolds almost imperceptibly. There is no hope of preserving the outer layers of paper, as these are always torn or rotten. You have to get down to a certain depth, when you reach the part of the manuscript that is only charred. Once a few columns have been unrolled, they are cut off and stuck onto a canvas support. It takes several months to unfold just one of these manuscripts, and in all the time since the work began, they have managed to save only the last thirty-eight columns of a Greek work condemning music. It is written by a certain Philodiorus, who is mentioned by Strabo and other ancient writers; his name and the subject of the book were fortunately discovered at the end of the manuscript. There are a few small gaps in the thirty-eight columns, but overall the writing is beautifully formed and clearly legible.

Two other columns from Greek manuscripts are on display; these were cut off before they discovered the secret of how to unroll them.

Count de Caylus

mansion, which has still not been fully excavated. They are made of Egyptian papyrus and are as black as coal. For a long while no one could think of a way of unrolling these papers, and, in their uncertainty, they decided to cut some of them in two lengthways, as if dividing a cylinder. This procedure allowed some of the writing to be seen quite clearly, but the manuscript as a whole was completely lost in the process. The numerous layers of papyrus were stuck together so tightly, that as they were detached, they were often reduced to dust. The most they

Italian Journeys

From the mid-18th century, artists and writers from all over the world set out for Italy, hoping to discover there both the experience of a new country and memories of antiquity.

A Visit to Pompeii and Herculaneum

Naples, Sunday 11 March 1787

As Tischbein and I drove to Pompeii, we saw on every hand many views which we knew well from drawings, but now they were all fitted together into one splendid landscape.

Pompeii surprises everyone by its compactness and its smallness of scale. The streets are narrow, though straight and provided with sidewalks, the houses small

The painter Johann Heinrich Tischbein, who accompanied Goethe on his travels in Italy, left us this portrait of the great writer to commemorate their discovery of the ancient world.

and windowless—their only light comes from their entrances and open arcades—and even the public buildings, the bench tomb at the town gate, the temple, and a villa nearby look more like architectural models or dolls' houses than real buildings. But their rooms, passages, and arcades are gaily painted. The walls have plain surfaces with richly detailed frescoes painted on them, most of which have now deteriorated. These frescoes are surrounded by amusing arabesques in admirable taste: from one, enchanting figures of children and nymphs evolve, in another, wild and tame animals emerge out of luxuriant floral wreaths.

Though the city, first buried under a rain of ashes and stones and then looted by the excavators, is now completely destroyed, it still bears witness to an artistic instinct and a love of art shared by a whole people, which even the most ardent art lover today can neither feel nor understand and desire.

Considering the distance between Pompeii and Vesuvius, the volcanic debris which buried the city cannot have been driven here, either by the explosive force of the eruption or by a strong wind: my own conjecture is that the stones and ashes must have remained suspended in the air for some time, like clouds, before they descended upon the unfortunate city....

To picture more clearly what must have happened historically one should think of a mountain village buried in snow. The spaces between the buildings, and even the buildings themselves, crushed under the weight of the fallen material, were buried and invisible, with perhaps a wall sticking up here and there; sooner or later, people took this mound over and planted vineyards and gardens on it. It was probably peasants digging on their allotments who made the first important treasure hauls.

Naples, Sunday 18 March 1787
We could not put off any longer going to see Herculaneum and the Portici museum of objects excavated there. Herculaneum lay at the foot of Vesuvius and was completely buried

under lava, to which subsequent eruptions added fresh layers, so that the ancient city is now sixty feet below ground level. It was discovered when, in the course of digging a well, some workmen came across floors of paved marble. It is a thousand pities that the site was not excavated methodically by German miners, instead of being casually ransacked as if by brigands, for many noble works of antiquity must have been thereby lost or ruined.

We descended a flight of sixty steps to a vault, where we admired by torchlight the former open-air theater, while the guard told us about the things that were found there and brought to the light of day.

We had good letters of recommendation to the museum and were well received, but we were not allowed to make any drawings. Perhaps this made us pay attention even more closely to what we saw, so that we were all the more vividly transported into the past, when all these objects were part and parcel of their owners' daily life. They quite changed my picture of Pompeii. In my mind's eye its homes now looked both more cramped and more spacious—more cramped because I now saw them crowded with objects, and more spacious because these objects were not made merely for use but were decorated with such art and grace that they enlarged and refreshed the mind in a way that the physical space of even the largest room cannot do.

There was one beautiful jar, for example, with an exquisitely wrought rim which, on closer inspection, turned out to be two hinged semicircular handles, by which the vessel could be lifted and carried with ease. The lamps are decorated with as many masks and scrolls of foliage as they have wicks, so that each flame illuminates a different work of art. There were high, slender bronze pedestals, evidently intended as lamp stands. The lamps which were suspended from the ceiling were hung with all sorts of cunningly wrought figures which surprise and delight the eye as they swing and dangle.

We followed the custodians from room to room, trying to enjoy and learn as much as possible in the little time we had. We hope to come back.

Johann Wolfgang Goethe
Italian Journey, 1786–8

Stendhal's Trip

Naples, 5 April 1817
As I was leaving the *Museum of Antique Painting* at Portici, I met with a trio of English naval officers, who were on their way in. Now, this Museum contains no less than two-and-twenty

rooms. On the road back into Naples, I kept up a steady gallop; yet before I reached the *ponte della Maddalena,* I was caught and overtaken by these same three English travelers, who, later in the evening, assured me that the paintings they had seen were positively *splendid,* and indeed one of the strangest sights in all the universe. The total time which they had spent inside the Museum amounted to somewhere between three and four minutes.

This collection, which affords such a treasure-house of curiosities for the true lover of art, consists of frescoes which have been removed from Pompeii and Herculaneum. They reveal a complete absence of *chiaroscuro,* a very limited range of color, a passable feeling for design and considerable facility. Two items in particular I found pleasing: *Orestes Recognized by Iphigenia in…*

Tauris, and *Theseus Thanked by the Young Athenians for Having Delivered Them from the Minotaur.* Both contain a wealth of noble simplicity, without a single theatrical gesture. The general impression is of a series of bad works by Domenichino, albeit further still removed from greatness by the presence of numerous faults of draftsmanship—errors which this fine artist would never have committed. There are to be observed at Portici, among a host of minor, half-obliterated frescoes, five or six major productions on the scale of Raphael's *Santa Cecilia.* Once upon a time, these frescoes served to ornament a bath-chamber at Herculaneum. Yet no one save a scholar could be so asinine as to claim that such stuff outweighs the quattrocento; in point of fact, it is nothing but a highly remarkable artistic curio.

Stendhal
Rome, Naples, and Florence, 1817

The Museo Borbonico

Most of the paintings of Pompeii and Herculaneum have been removed to the Museo at Naples. These consist principally of mural decorations, and generally without perspective, there being one or two figures on a dark background, with now and then animals, slight landscape views, and sections of architecture. The coloring is feeble, it being scarcely more than indicated, or rather subdued, effaced, and not by time (for I have seen quite fresh pictures), but designedly. To attract the eye was not an aim in these somewhat somber apartments; they delighted in an attitude or form of the body, the mind being entertained with healthy and poetic images of physical activity. I have derived more pleasure from these paintings than from the most celebrated of the Renaissance epoch. There is more nature, more life in them.

The subjects have no particular interest, consisting ordinarily of a male or female figure nearly nude, raising an arm or a leg; Mars and Venus, Diana finding Endymion, Briseis conducted by Agamemnon, and the like, dancers, fauns, centaurs, a warrior bearing away a female, who, so carried, is so much at her ease! Nothing more is requisite, because you feel at once their beauty and repose. You cannot comprehend, before seeing it, how many charming attitudes a half-draped figure, floating in the air, can present to you; how many ways a veil can be raised, a

When he visited Italy Stendhal was more interested in contemporary customs than in antiquities, as we can tell from his comments on Pompeian painting.

The subject of one of the frescoes described by Taine: Briseis, the young captive loved by Achilles, is carried off by Agamemnon.

flowing tunic arranged, a limb projected, and a breast exposed. The painters of these pictures enjoyed a unique advantage, one which no others have possessed, even those of the Renaissance, of living amid congenial social customs, of constantly seeing figures naked and draped in the amphitheater and in the baths, and besides this, of cultivating the corporeal endowments of strength and fleetness of foot. They alluded to fine breasts, well-set necks, and muscular arms as we of the present day do to expressive countenances and well-cut pantaloons.

The first and most enduring is the image of the reddish-grey city, half ruined and deserted, a pile of stones on a hill of rocks, with rows of thick wall, and bluish flagging glittering in the dazzling white atmosphere; and surrounding this the sea, the mountains, and an infinite perspective.

On the summit stand the temples,

that of Justice, of Venus, of Augustus, of Mercury, the house of Eumachia, and other temples, still incomplete, and, farther on, also on an elevation, the temple of Neptune. They also raised their gods on high in the pure atmosphere, of itself a divinity. The forum and the curia alongside afford a noble spot for councils, and to offer sacrifices. In the distance you discern the grand lines of the vapory mountains, the tranquil tops of the Italian pine; then to the east, within the blonde sunlit haze, fine tree-forms and diversities of culture. You turn, and but little effort of the imagination enables you to reconstruct these temples. These columns, these Corinthian capitals, this simple arrangement, those openings of blue between those marble shafts, what an impression such a spectacle contemplated from infancy left on the mind! The city in those days was a veritable patrimony, and not, as now, a government collection of lodging-houses....

All these streets are narrow; the greater portion are mere lanes, over which one strides with ease. Generally there is room only for a cart, and ruts are still visible: from time to time wide stones afford a crossing like a bridge. These details indicate other customs than our own; there was evidently no great traffic as in our cities, nothing like our heavily-loaded vehicles, and fast-trotting fanciful carriages. Their carts transported grain, oil, and provisions: much of the transportation was done on the arm and by slaves: the rich traveled about in litters. They possessed fewer and different conveniences. One prominent trait of antique civilization is the absence of industrial pursuits. All supplies, utensils, and tissues, everything that machines and free labor now produce in such enormous quantities for everybody and at every price, were wanting to them. It was the slave who turned the mill-wheel: man devoted himself to the beautiful, and not to the useful; producing but little, he could consume but little. Life was necessarily simple.... A few thousands of proud, brave, temperate men..., who delighted in the view of a hill with a group of beautiful temples and statues, who entertained themselves with public business, and passed their days in the gymnasium, at the forum, in the baths and the theater, who... were content with things as they stood;—such was the city of antiquity

Almost everywhere in the center of the house is a garden like a large saloon, and in the middle of this a marble basin, a fountain flowing into it, and the whole enclosed within a portico of columns. What could be more charming, and simple, and better disposed for the warm hours of the day? With green leaves visible between two white columns, red tiles against the blue of the sky, the murmuring water sparkling among flowers like a jet of liquid pearls, and those shadows of porticoes intersected by the powerful light; is there a more congenial place for the body to grow freely, for healthy meditation, and to enjoy, without ostentation or affectation, all that is most beautiful in nature and in life? Some of these fountains bear lions' heads, dogs, and fauns grouped around their margins. In the most capacious of all these houses, that of Diomed, orange and lemon trees, similar, probably, to those of ancient days, are putting forth their fresh green buds; a fishpool gleams brightly, and a small colonnade encloses a summer dining-room, the whole embraced within the

Hippolyte Taine (1828–93) discovered Italy in the 1860s. As a historian, he aimed to place its people and monuments in their historical context.

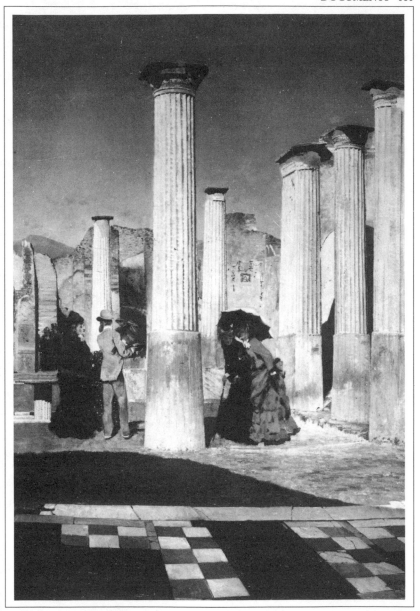

square of a grand portico. The more the imagination dwells on the social economy of antiquity, the more beautiful it seems, and the more conformable to the climate and the nature of man. The women had their *gynaeceum* in the rear behind the court and portico, a secluded retreat with no external communication, and entirely separated from public life. They were not very active in their small apartments; they indulged in indolent repose, like Italian ladies of the present day, or employed themselves on woolen fabrics, awaiting a father's or husband's return from the business and converse of men. Wandering eyes passed carelessly over obscure walls, dimly discerning, not pictures, as in our day, plastering them, not archaeological curiosities, and works of a different art and country; but figures repeating and beautifying ordinary attitudes, such as retiring to and arising from bed, the siesta, and various avocations; goddesses surrounding Paris, a Fortune, slender and elegant, like the females of Primaticcio, or a Deidamia frightened and falling backward on a chair.

The theater crowns the summit of a hill; its seats are of Parian marble; in front is Vesuvius, and the sea radiant with morning splendor. Its roof was an awning, which, again, was sometimes wanting. Compare this with our nocturnal edifices, lighted by gas and filled with a mephitic atmosphere, where people pile themselves up in gaudy boxes ranged in rows like suspended cages; you then appreciate the difference between a gymnastic natural life with athletic forms, and our complicated artificial life with its dress-coats. The impression is the same in the majestic amphitheater exposed to the sun, except that here is the blot of antique society, the Roman imprint of blood. The same impression you find in the baths; the red cornice of the *frigidarium* is full of charming airy little cupids, bounding away on horses or conducting chariots. Nothing is more agreeable and better understood than the drying room, with its vault covered with small figures in relief in rich medallions, and a file of Hercules ranged round the wall, their vigorous shoulders supporting the entablature. All these forms live and are healthy; none are exaggerated or overloaded. What a contrast on comparing with this our modern bathhouse, with its artificial, insipid nudities, its sentimental and voluptuous designs. The bathhouse nowadays is a washroom; in former times it was a pleasant retreat and a gymnastic institution. Several hours of the day were devoted to it: the muscles got to be supple and the skin brilliant; man here savored the voluptuous animality which permeated his alternately braced and mollified flesh; he lived not only through the head, as now, but through the body.

We descend and leave the city by the Street of Tombs. These tombs are almost entire; nothing can be nobler than their forms, nothing more solemn without being lugubrious. Death was not then surrounded with the torments of ascetic superstition, with ideas of hell; in the mind of the ancients it was one of the *offices* of man, simply a termination of life, a serious and not a terrible thing, which one regarded calmly and not with the shuddering doubts of Hamlet. The ashes and images of their ancestors were preserved in their dwellings; they saluted them on entering, and the living maintained intercourse with them; at the entrance of a city tombs were ranged on both sides of the street, and seemed to be the primitive, the original city of its founders. Hippias, in one of Plato's dialogues, says that "that which is most beautiful for a man is to be rich, healthy, and honored by Greeks, to attain old age, to pay funeral honors to his parents when they die, and himself to receive from his children a fitting and magnificent burial."

The truest history would be that of the five or six ideas that rule in the mind of man—how an ordinary man, two thousand years ago, regarded death, fame, well-being, country, love, and happiness. Two ideas controlled ancient civilization; the first, that of man, and the second, that of the city: to fashion a fine animal, agile, temperate, brave, hardy, and complete, and this through physical exercise and selection of good stock; and then to construct a small exclusive community, containing in its bosom all that man loved and respected, a kind of permanent camp with the exigences of continual danger;—these were the two ideas that gave birth to all the rest.

Hippolyte Taine
Travels in Italy, 1865

The Macabre and the Beautiful

Charles Dickens spent nearly a year in Italy, in 1844–5. Pompeii's mixture of the macabre and the beautiful appealed strongly to his imagination, always fascinated by the thought of sudden death.

Stand at the bottom of the great market-place of Pompeii, and look up the silent streets, through the ruined temples of Jupiter and Isis, over the broken houses with their inmost sanctuaries open to the day, away to Mount Vesuvius, bright and snowy in the peaceful distance; and lose all count of time, and heed of other things, in the strange and melancholy sensation of seeing the Destroyed and the Destroyer making this quiet picture in the sun. Then, ramble on, and see, at every turn, the little familiar tokens of human habitation and every-day pursuits; the chafing of the bucket-rope in the stone rim of the exhausted well; the track of carriage-wheels in the pavement of the street; the marks of drinking-vessels on the stone counter of the wine-shop; the amphorae in private cellars, stored away so many hundred years ago, and undisturbed to this hour—all rendering the solitude and deadly lonesomeness of the place, ten thousand times more solemn, than if the volcano, in its fury, had swept the city from the earth, and sunk it in the bottom of the sea.

After it was shaken by the earthquake which preceded the eruption, workmen were employed in shaping out, in stone, new ornaments for temples and other buildings that had suffered. Here lies their work, outside the city gate, as if they would return to-morrow.

In the cellar of Diomede's house, where certain skeletons were found

huddled together, close to the door, the impression of their bodies on the ashes, hardened with the ashes, and became stamped and fixed there, after they had shrunk, inside, to scanty bones. So, in the theatre of Herculaneum, a comic mask, floating on the stream when it was hot and liquid, stamped its mimic features in it as it hardened into stone; and now, it turns upon the stranger the fantastic look it turned upon the audiences in that same theatre two thousand years ago.

Next to the wonder of going up and down the streets, and in and out of the houses, and traversing the secret chambers of the temples of a religion that has vanished from the earth, and finding so many fresh traces of remote antiquity: as if the course of Time had been stopped after this desolation, and there had been no nights and days, months, years, and centuries, since: nothing is more impressive and terrible than the many evidences of the searching nature of the ashes, as bespeaking their irresistible power, and the impossibility of escaping them. In the wine-cellars, they forced their way into the earthen vessels: displacing the wine and choking them, to the brim, with dust. In the tombs, they forced the ashes of the dead from the funeral urns, and rained new ruin even into them. The mouths, and eyes, and skulls of all the skeletons, were stuffed with this terrible hail. In Herculaneum, where the flood was of a different and a heavier kind, it rolled in, like a sea. Imagine a deluge of water turned to marble, at its height—and that is what is called "the lava" here.

Many of the paintings on the walls in the roofless chambers of both cities, or carefully removed to the museum at

Naples, are as fresh and plain, as if they had been executed yesterday. Here are subjects of still life, as provisions, dead game, bottles, glasses, and the like; familiar classical stories, or mythological fables, always forcibly and plainly told; conceits of cupids, quarrelling, sporting, working at trades; theatrical rehearsals; poets reading their productions to their friends; inscriptions chalked upon the walls; political squibs, advertisements, rough drawings by schoolboys; everything to people and restore the ancient cities, in the fancy of their wondering visitor....

The least among these objects lends its aid to swell the interest of Vesuvius, and invest it with a perfect fascination. The looking, from either ruined city, into the neighbouring grounds overgrown with beautiful vines and luxuriant trees; and remembering that house upon house, temple on temple, building after building, and street after street, are still lying underneath the roots of all the quiet cultivation, waiting to be turned up to the light of day; is something so wonderful, so full of mystery, so captivating to the imagination, that one would think it would be paramount, and yield to nothing else. To nothing but Vesuvius; but the mountain is the genius of the scene. From every indication of the ruin it has worked, we look, again, with an absorbing interest to where its smoke is rising up into the sky. It is beyond us, as we thread the ruined streets; above us, as we stand upon the ruined walls; we follow it through every vista of broken columns, as we wander through the empty court-yards of the houses; and through the garlandings and interlacings of every wanton vine. Turning away to Paestum yonder, to

see the awful structures built, the least aged of them, hundreds of years before the birth of Christ, and standing yet, erect in lonely majesty, upon the wild, malaria-blighted plain—we watch Vesuvius as it disappears from the prospect, and watch for it again, on our return, with the same thrill of interest: as the doom and destiny of all this beautiful country, biding its terrible time.

Charles Dickens
Pictures from Italy, 1845

In "Pom-*pay*-e"

Mark Twain, who worked as a journalist before becoming a novelist, joined a group of American tourists for a tour of the Mediterranean. After visiting the Holy Land and Egypt, he and his traveling companions found themselves in Pompeii.

They pronounce it Pom-*pay*-e. I always had an idea that you went down into Pompeii with torches, by the way of damp, dark stairways, just as you do in silver mines, and traversed gloomy tunnels with lava overhead and something on either hand like dilapidated prisons gouged out of the solid earth, that faintly resembled houses. But you do nothing of the kind. Fully one-half of the buried city, perhaps, is completely exhumed and thrown open freely to the light of day; and there stand the long rows of solidly-built brick houses (roofless) just as they stood eighteen hundred years ago, hot with the flaming sun; and there lie their floors, clean-swept, and not a bright fragment tarnished or wanting of the labored mosaics that pictured them with the beasts, and birds, and flowers which we copy in perishable carpets to-day; and there are the Venuses, and Bacchuses, and Adonises, making love and getting drunk in many-hued frescoes on the walls of saloon and bed-chamber; and there are the narrow streets and narrower sidewalks, paved with flags of good hard lava, the one deeply rutted with the chariot-wheels, and the other with the passing feet of the Pompeiians of by-gone centuries; and there are the bake-shops, the temples, the halls of justice, the baths, the theatres—all clean-scraped and neat, and suggesting nothing of the nature of a silver mine away down in the bowels of the earth. The broken pillars lying about, the doorless doorways and the crumbled tops of the wilderness of walls, were

wonderfully suggestive of the "burnt district" in one of our cities, and if there had been any charred timbers, shattered windows, heaps of debris, and general blackness and smokiness about the place, the resemblance would have been perfect. But no—the sun shines as brightly down on old Pompeii to-day as it did when Christ was born in Bethlehem, and its streets are cleaner a hundred times than ever Pompeiian saw them in her prime. I know whereof I speak—for in the great, chief thoroughfares (Merchant Street and the Street of Fortune) have I not seen with my own eyes how for two hundred years at least the pavements were not repaired! —how ruts five and even ten inches deep were worn into the thick flagstones by the chariot-wheels of generations of swindled tax-payers? And do I not know by these signs that Street Commissioners of Pompeii never attended to their business, and that if they never mended the pavements they never cleaned them? And, besides, is it not the inborn nature of Street Commissioners to avoid their duty whenever they get a chance? I wish I knew the name of the last one that held office in Pompeii so that I could give him a blast. I speak with feeling on this subject, because I caught my foot in one of those ruts, and the sadness that came over me when I saw the first poor skeleton, with ashes and lava sticking to it, was tempered by the reflection that may be that party was the Street Commissioner.…

Then we lounged through many and many a sumptuous private mansion which we could not have entered without a formal invitation in incomprehensible Latin, in the olden time, when the owners lived there—

and we probably wouldn't have got it. These people built their houses a good deal alike. The floors were laid in fanciful figures wrought in mosaics of many-colored marbles. At the threshold your eyes fall upon a Latin sentence of welcome, sometimes, or a picture of a dog, with the legend "Beware of the Dog," and sometimes a picture of a bear or a faun with no inscription at all. Then you enter a sort of vestibule, where they used to keep the hat-rack, I suppose; next a room with a large marble basin in the midst and the pipes of a fountain; on either side are bedrooms; beyond the fountain is a reception-room, then a little garden, dining-room, and so forth and so on. The floors were all mosaic, the walls were stuccoed, or frescoed, or ornamented with bas-reliefs, and here and there were statues, large and small, and little fish-pools, and cascades of sparkling water that sprang from secret places in the colonnade of handsome pillars that surrounded the court, and kept the flower-beds fresh and the air cool....

It was a quaint and curious pastime, wandering through this old silent city of the dead—lounging through utterly deserted streets where thousands and thousands of human beings once bought and sold, and walked and rode, and made the place resound with the noise and confusion of traffic and pleasure. They were not lazy. They hurried in those days. We had evidence of that. There was a temple on one corner, and it was a shorter cut to go between the columns of that temple from one street to the other than to go around—and behold that pathway had been worn deep into the heavy flag-stone floor of the building by generations of time-saving feet! They

would not go around when it was quicker to go through. We do that way in our cities.

Everywhere, you see things that make you wonder how old these old houses were before the night of destruction came—things, too, which bring back those long dead inhabitants and place them living before your eyes. For instance: The steps (two feet thick—lava blocks) that lead up out of the school, and the same kind of steps that lead up into the dress circle of the principal theatre, are almost worn through! For ages the boys hurried out of that school, and for ages their parents hurried into that theatre, and the nervous feet that have been dust and ashes for eighteen centuries have left their record for us to read to-day....

And so I turned away and went through shop after shop and store after store, far down the long street of the

"At the threshold your eyes fall upon a Latin sentence [meaning]... 'Beware of the Dog.'"

merchants, and called for the wares of Rome and the East, but the tradesmen were gone, the marts were silent, and nothing was left but the broken jars all set in cement of cinders and ashes....

In a bake-shop... the exhumers of Pompeii found nice, well baked loaves which the baker had not found time to remove from the ovens the last time he left his shop, because circumstances compelled him to leave in such a hurry.

In one house (the only building in Pompeii which no woman is now allowed to enter) were the small rooms and short beds of solid masonry, just as they were in the old times, and on the walls were pictures which looked almost as fresh as if they were painted yesterday, but which no pen could have the hardihood to describe; and here and there were Latin inscriptions—obscene scintillations of wit, scratched by hands that possibly were uplifted to Heaven for succor in the midst of a driving storm of fire before the night was done.

In one of the principal streets was a ponderous stone tank, and a water-spout that supplied it, and where the tired, heated toilers from the Campagna used to rest their right hands when they bent over to put their lips to the spout, the thick stone was worn down to a broad groove an inch or two deep. Think of the countless thousands of hands that had pressed that spot in the ages that are gone, to so reduce a stone that is as hard as iron!

They had a great public bulletin board in Pompeii—a place where announcements for gladiatorial combats, elections, and such things, were posted—not on perishable paper, but carved in enduring stone. One lady, who, I take it, was rich and well brought up, advertised a dwelling or so

to rent, with baths and all the modern improvements, and several hundred shops, stipulating that the dwellings should not be put to immoral purposes....

In one of these long Pompeiian halls the skeleton of a man was found, with ten pieces of gold in one hand and a large key in the other. He had seized his money and started toward the door, but the fiery tempest caught him at the very threshold, and he sank down and died. One more minute of precious time would have saved him. I saw the skeletons of a man, a woman, and two young girls. The woman had her hands spread wide apart, as if in mortal terror, and I imagined I could still trace upon her shapeless face something of the expression of wild despair that distorted it when the heavens rained fire in these streets, so many ages ago. The girls and the man lay with their faces upon their arms, as if they had tried to shield them from the enveloping cinders. In one

The tourists, eager for excitement, climbed Vesuvius after visiting the city destroyed by the terrible volcano.

apartment eighteen skeletons were found, all in sitting postures, and blackened places on the walls still mark their shapes and show their attitudes, like shadows. One of them, a woman, still wore upon her skeleton throat a necklace, with her name engraved upon it—JULIE DI DIOMEDE.

But perhaps the most poetical thing Pompeii has yielded to modern research, was that grand figure of a Roman soldier, clad in complete armor; who, true to his duty, true to his proud name of a soldier of Rome, and full of the stern courage which had given to that name its glory, stood to his post by the city gate, erect and unflinching, till the hell that raged around him *burned out* the dauntless spirit it could not conquer....

We came out from under the solemn mysteries of this city of the Venerable Past—this city which perished, with all its old ways and its quaint old fashions about it, remote centuries ago, when the Disciples were preaching the new religion, which is as old as the hills to us now—and went dreaming among the trees that grow over acres and acres of its still buried streets and squares, till a shrill whistle and the cry of *"All aboard—last train for Naples!"* woke me up and reminded me that I belonged in the nineteenth century, and was not a dusty mummy, caked with ashes and cinders, eighteen hundred years old. The transition was startling. The idea of a railroad train actually running to old dead Pompeii, and whistling irreverently, and calling for passengers in the most bustling and business-like way, was as strange a thing as one could imagine, and as unpoetical and disagreeable as it was strange.

Mark Twain
The Innocents Abroad, 1875

The Last Days of Pompeii

In Edward Bulwer-Lytton's dramatic reconstruction of the final moments of Pompeii, the central characters, the lovers Glaucus and Ione, flee as a burning cloud of ash descends upon the city.

The Progress of the Destruction

The cloud, which had scattered so deep a murkiness over the day, had now settled into a solid and impenetrable mass. It resembled less even the thickest gloom of a night in the open air than the close and blind darkness of some narrow room. But in proportion as the blackness gathered, did the lightnings around Vesuvius increase in their vivid and scorching glare. Nor was their horrible beauty confined to the usual hues of fire; no rainbow ever rivalled their varying and prodigal dyes. Now brightly blue as the most azure depth of a southern sky—now of a livid and snakelike green, darting restlessly to and fro as the folds of an enormous serpent—now of a lurid and intolerable crimson, gushing forth through the columns of smoke, far and wide, and lighting up the whole city from arch to arch,—then suddenly dying into a sickly paleness, like the ghost of their own life!

In the pauses of the showers, you heard the rumbling of the earth beneath, and the groaning waves of the tortured sea; or, lower still, and audible but to the watch of intensest fear, the grinding and hissing murmur of the escaping gases through the chasms of the distant mountain. Sometimes the cloud appeared to break from its solid mass, and, by the lightning, to assume quaint and vast mimicries of human or of monster shapes, striding across the gloom, hurtling one upon the other, and vanishing swiftly into the turbulent abyss of shade; so that, to the eyes and fancies of the affrighted wanderers, the unsubstantial vapours were as the bodily forms of gigantic foes,—the agents of terror and of death.

The ashes in many places were already knee-deep; and the boiling showers which came from the steaming breath of the volcano forced their way into the houses, bearing with them a strong and suffocating vapour. In some places, immense fragments of rock, hurled upon the house roofs, bore down along the streets masses of confused ruin, which yet more and more, with every hour, obstructed the way; and, as the day advanced, the motion of the earth was more sensibly felt—the footing seemed to slide and creep—nor could chariot or litter be kept steady, even on the most level ground.

Sometimes the huger stones striking against each other as they fell, broke into countless fragments, emitting sparks of fire, which caught whatever was combustible within their reach; and along the plains beyond the city the darkness was now terribly relieved; for several houses, and even vineyards, had been set on flames; and at various intervals the fires rose suddenly and fiercely against the solid gloom. To add to this partial relief of the darkness, the citizens had, here and there, in the more public places, such as the porticos of temples and the entrances to the forum, endeavoured to place rows of torches; but these rarely continued long; the showers and the winds extinguished them, and the sudden darkness into which their sudden birth was converted had something in it doubly terrible and doubly impressing on the impotence of human hopes, the lesson of despair.

Frequently, by the momentary light of these torches, parties of fugitives encountered each other, some hurrying towards the sea, others flying from the sea back to the land, for the ocean had retreated rapidly from the shore—an utter darkness lay over it, and upon its groaning and tossing waves the storm of cinders and rock fell without the protection which the streets and roofs afforded to the land. Wild—haggard—ghastly with supernatural fears, these groups encountered each other, but without the leisure to speak, to consult, to advise; for the showers fell now frequently, though not continuously, extinguishing the lights, which showed to each band the deathlike faces of the other, and hurrying all to seek refuge beneath the nearest shelter. The whole elements of civilization were broken up....

Through this awful scene did the Athenian wade his way, accompanied by Ione and the blind girl. Suddenly, a rush of hundreds, in their path to the sea, swept by them. Nydia was torn from the side of Glaucus, who, with Ione, was borne rapidly onward; and when the crowd (whose forms they saw not, so thick was the gloom) were gone, Nydia was still separated from their side. Glaucus shouted her name. No answer came. They retraced their steps—in vain: they could not discover her—it was evident that she had been swept along some opposite direction by the human current. Their friend, their preserver, was lost! And hitherto Nydia had been their guide. *Her blindness rendered the scene familiar to her alone.* Accustomed, through a perpetual night, to thread the windings of the city, she had led them unerringly towards the sea-shore, by which they had resolved to hazard an escape. Now, which way could they wend? all was rayless to them—a maze without a clue. Wearied, despondent, bewildered, they, however, passed along, the ashes falling upon their heads, the fragmentary stones dashing up in sparkles before their feet.

"Alas! alas!" murmured Ione, "I can go no farther, my steps sink among the scorching cinders. Fly, dearest!—beloved, fly! and leave me to my fate!"

"Hush, my betrothed! my bride! Death with thee is sweeter than life without thee! Yet, whither—oh! whither, can we direct ourselves through the gloom? Already it seems that we have made but a circle, and are in the very spot which we quitted an hour ago."

"O gods! yon rock—see, it hath riven the roof before us! It is death to move through the streets!"

"Blessed lightning! See, Ione—see! the portico of the Temple of Fortune is before us. Let us creep beneath it; it will protect us from the showers."

He caught his beloved in his arms, and with difficulty and labour gained the temple. He bore her to the remoter and more sheltered part of the portico, and leaned over her, that he might shield her, with his own form, from the lightning and the showers! The beauty and the unselfishness of love could hallow even that dismal time!

"Who is there?" said the trembling and hollow voice of one who had preceded them in their place of refuge. "Yet, what matters?—the crush of the ruined world forbids to us friends or foes."

Ione turned at the sound of the voice, and, with a faint shriek, cowered again beneath the arms of Glaucus: and he, looking in the direction of the voice, beheld the cause of her alarm. Through the darkness glared forth two burning eyes—the lightning flashed and lingered athwart the temple—and

Glaucus, with a shudder, perceived the lion to which he had been doomed couched beneath the pillars;—and, close beside it, unwitting of the vicinity, lay the giant form of him who had accosted them—the wounded gladiator, Niger.

That lightning had revealed to each other the form of beast and man; yet the instinct of both was quelled. Nay, the lion crept nearer and nearer to the gladiator, as for companionship; and the gladiator did not recede or tremble. The revolution of Nature had dissolved her lighter terrors as well as her wonted ties.

While they were thus terribly protected, a group of men and women, bearing torches, passed by the temple. They were of the congregation of the Nazarenes; and a sublime and unearthly emotion had not, indeed, quelled their awe, but it had robbed awe of fear. They had long believed, according to the error of the early Christians, that the Last Day was at hand; they imagined now that the Day had come.

"Woe! woe!" cried, in a shrill and piercing voice, the elder at their head. "Behold! the Lord descendeth to judgment! He maketh fire come down from heaven in the sight of men! Woe! woe! ye strong and mighty! Woe to ye of the fasces and the purple! Woe to the idolater and the worshipper of the beast! Woe to ye who pour forth the blood of saints, and gloat over the death-pangs of the sons of God! Woe to the harlot of the sea!—woe! woe!"

And with a loud and deep chorus, the troop chanted forth along the wild horrors of the air,—"Woe to the harlot of the sea!—woe! woe!"

The Nazarenes paced slowly on, their torches still flickering in the storm,

"Frequently, by the momentary light of these torches, parties of fugitives encountered each other, some hurrying towards the sea, others flying from the sea back to the land."

their voices still raised in menace and solemn warning, till, lost amid the windings in the streets, the darkness of the atmosphere and the silence of death again fell over the scene.

There was one of the frequent pauses in the showers, and Glaucus encouraged Ione once more to proceed. Just as they stood, hesitating, on the last step of the portico, an old man, with a bag in his right hand and leaning upon a youth, tottered by. The youth bore a torch. Glaucus recognised the two as father and son—miser and prodigal.

"Father," said the youth, "if you cannot move more swiftly, I must leave you, or we *both* perish!"

"Fly, boy, then, and leave thy sire!"

"But I cannot fly to starve; give me thy bag of gold!" And the youth snatched at it.

"Wretch! wouldst thou rob thy father?"

"Ay! who can tell the tale in this hour? Miser, perish!"

The boy struck the old man to the ground, plucked the bag from his relaxing hand, and fled onward with a shrill yell.

"Ye gods!" cried Glaucus: "are ye blind, then, even in the dark? Such crimes may well confound the guiltless with the guilty in one common ruin. Ione, on!—on!"…

Advancing, as men grope for escape in a dungeon, Ione and her lover continued their uncertain way. At moments when the volcanic lightnings lingered over the streets, they were enabled, by that awful light, to steer and guide their progress: yet, little did the view it presented to them cheer or encourage their path.…clear and distinct through all were the mighty and various sounds from the Fatal Mountain; its rushing winds; its whirling torrents; and, from time to time, the burst and roar of some more fiery and fierce explosion.

Edward Bulwer-Lytton
The Last Days of Pompeii, 1834

A Pompeian Fantasy

The main character in Wilhelm Jensen's novella Gradiva *is an archaeologist called Norbert Hanold. Standing in front of a bas-relief carving that shows a young girl, Gradiva, walking, the doctor falls into a deep, dreamlike state. Freud interpreted the novella, reading the whole thing as if it were a patient's account. He believed that, like every archaeologist, Hanold dreamed he was witnessing the catastrophic events firsthand.*

In his dream, Dr. Hanold finds himself face to face with Gradiva, in Pompeii, on 24 August 79. He then realizes that this young girl is none other than a childhood friend to whom he had never paid much attention. Her name is Zoë Bertgang, Zoë meaning "life."

He suddenly caught a glimpse of Gradiva, right in front of him, looking exactly as she had the day before, wearing the same clothes, and sitting on the same step between the same two yellow columns. He refused to allow himself to be deceived by this product of his imagination.... Even so, he could not help gazing at the insubstantial vision that he had conjured up. He stood rooted to the spot, and almost before he realized he was speaking, there fell from his lips, in an agonized tone, the words: "Oh! if only you were still alive, still existed!"

He fell silent, and there was not even a breath of wind to disturb the hush that once more descended on the ruins of the old hall. Until all at once another voice broke the empty stillness, saying: "Wouldn't you prefer to sit down? You look tired."

Norbert Hanold's heart missed a beat. He gathered together in his head as much sense as he could muster: a vision was incapable of speech. Or were his ears also playing tricks on him? He stared at her, leaning his hand on a column to steady himself.

The voice again asked him a question, and that voice could only be Gradiva's: "Have you brought the white flower for me?"

He was gripped by a feeling of dizziness; realizing that he would have to sit down, as his legs could no longer support him, he allowed himself to slide down onto a step, until he was sitting opposite her, leaning against a column. She stared at him with her clear gaze, but the look in her eyes was quite different from the one she had given him the day before, when she had suddenly got up and left him. All trace of denial and displeasure had disappeared from her expression, as if she had since changed her opinion of him, and in their place was a searching curiosity and a desire to find out more....As he had still not answered her question, however, she spoke again, and said: "Yesterday you told me that you had once called out to me as I was lying down to go to sleep, and that you had afterwards remained standing next to me; my face turned as white as marble, you said. When and where did this happen? I cannot remember such an incident, and I beg you to explain what happened in more detail."

Norbert had by now regained sufficient control over his speech to be able to answer: "It was night; you sat down on the steps of the Temple of Apollo in the Forum and the falling ashes from Vesuvius began to cover you."

"Ah!—so that's when it was. Yes, that is true—I had forgotten. But I should have realized it would be something of that kind. When you mentioned it yesterday, it was all so unexpected; I was startled. But, if I am not mistaken, that happened almost two thousand years ago. Were you alive then? You don't look that old to me."

She spoke quite seriously; only towards the end of this speech did a slight, infinitely gentle smile play around the corners of her mouth. Norbert felt embarrassed and uncertain, and stuttered a little as he replied: "No, I think in fact I had not yet been born

at that point, in A.D. 79—perhaps it was—yes, it must have been the state of mind that people call dreaming which carried me back to the time of the destruction of Pompeii. But I recognized you at first sight...."

A look of astonishment passed over the face of the young woman, who was sitting only a few steps away from him, and she repeated in a tone of wonder: "You recognized me? In your dream? How?"

"Initially, by the way you walk"

"You noticed that? Is there something special about my walk, then?"

Her amazement had visibly increased still further. He answered: "Yes—are you not conscious of it yourself? You walk with more grace than anyone I have ever seen, or at least, than anyone alive today. But I also recognized you straight away by everything else: your face and figure, your bearing and your clothes. Because everything exactly matches your bas-relief portrait in Rome."

"Ah! I see...," she replied once more in the same tone, "with my bas-relief portrait in Rome. I hadn't thought of that. And to be quite honest, I still don't entirely follow—what does it look like?—and have you seen it there?"

He then told her how, many years before, he had been fascinated by this relief and had been overjoyed to get hold of a plaster cast of it, which had been hanging in his room in Germany ever since. He looked at it every day, and he had become convinced that the picture represented a young girl from Pompeii, walking along over the flagstones of a street in her native city. This had been confirmed by his dream, and he now knew that it was also this dream that had forced him to travel here and find out whether he could discover any trace of her. At noon on the previous day, as he was standing on the corner of the Via del Mercurio, she had suddenly walked by before his very eyes, looking exactly as she did in her picture. She had seemed about to go into the House of Apollo, but a little farther on she had crossed the road again and disappeared in front of the House of Meleager.

She nodded and said: "Yes, I was intending to visit the House of Apollo, but then I came here instead."

He continued: "This made me think of the Greek poet Meleager, and I thought you might be one of his descendants, returning... to the house of your ancestor. But when I spoke to you in Greek, you didn't understand me."

"So that was Greek, was it? No, I don't speak it, or I have forgotten it, at least. But when you came back today, I heard you say something that I did understand. You expressed the wish that someone might still be there and alive. Only I didn't know who you meant."

He replied that, when he had first seen her, he was convinced that it was not really her, but a figment of his imagination, an illusion that showed her sitting at the same spot where he had met her the day before. She smiled at this and answered: "It would seem you have good reason to protect yourself from your excessively active imagination, though I would not have suspected it from the conversations we have had together." Then she broke off, and continued: "What is it about my walk, that you mentioned earlier?"

Clearly, she had developed an intense interest that would not allow her to abandon this point. He began: "Would you mind...?"

But all at once he paused, as he remembered anxiously that the day before, when he had asked her if she would lie down and sleep on the steps again, as she had done at the Temple of Apollo, she had abruptly stood up and walked away.... Now, though, she continued to gaze at him with a calm and untroubled expression of sympathy, and as he did not go on, she said: "It was kind of you to have me in mind, when you wished that someone could still be alive. Because of that, I will gladly do whatever you ask me to."

Norbert's fears were allayed by these words, and he replied: "It would make me very happy if I could see you walk by me the way you do in that relief...."

Without replying, she eagerly stood up and walked a little way between the wall and the row of columns. Her light and flowing gait resembled precisely the one that had impressed itself so clearly on his mind, the sole of her foot being lifted off the ground almost vertically with each step. But as he watched, Norbert realized for the first time that she was wearing light, sand-colored shoes of fine leather beneath her short dress, rather than sandals. When she returned and sat down again in silence, he began in spite of himself to speak of the fact that her shoes were not the same as the ones in the relief. At this, she replied: "Time changes everything, and sandals are unsuited to modern times; I wear shoes because they provide better protection from the dust and rain. But why did you ask me to walk in front of you? Is there something special about my walk?"...

Norbert explained that it had something to do with the way in which, been completely lost to them:—with one possible exception: a woman who had once seemed to him to walk in this way. Naturally, he had been unable to confirm this at the time, because of the crowds of people milling around her....

"What a pity!" she answered, "for if you had been able to confirm it, the information would have been of great scientific significance, and if you had succeeded in establishing it then, you would not have had to make the long journey here. But who is it you are talking about? Who is this Gradiva?"

"It was the name I gave to your portrait, because I didn't know your real name—and I still don't."

These last words were added rather tentatively, and she also hesitated a little before responding to his implied question: "My name is Zoë."

He exclaimed in a voice full of pain: "The name suits you perfectly, but to me it has a ring of bitter irony, for Zoë means 'life.'"

"We must accept the inevitable," she answered, "and I long ago grew used to the idea of being dead. My time has come to an end for today. You brought the flower of death for me,... so let me take it."

Rising to her feet, she stretched out her delicate hand, and he offered her the stem of asphodel, taking care not to touch her fingers. Accepting the flower-covered stem, she said: "Thank you. In spring people give roses to those who are more fortunate; but it is right that you should give me the flower of forget-fulness...." With this, she walked away and vanished at the corner of the portico, just as she had done the previous day, as if the earth had swallowed her up.

Wilhelm Jensen
Gradiva, 1903

when she took a step forward, the back foot was raised almost vertically off the ground; he added that he had spent several weeks, in the streets of his native town, trying to study the way modern women walked, but it appeared that this beautiful manner of moving had

The "Regime" of Amedeo Maiuri

Only in recent times has the rigorous approach of modern archaeologists enabled the excavations, the restoration, and protection of Pompeii to be organized on a scientific basis. During his long period of work at the site Maiuri gave the city its definitive appearance.

His thirty-seven years in charge of the excavations at Pompeii, between 1924 and 1961, enabled Amedeo Maiuri to benefit from an exceptional period of continuity. This great scholar developed a scientific approach that perfected our knowledge of the buried city by excavating the lower levels of the site to provide new and illuminating evidence of its historical development. He also had greater success than some of his predecessors in restoring houses that had been excavated at various times in the past.

From 1924 to 1941 he concentrated on the area around the Via dell' Abbondanza, his main aim being to uncover the *insulae* on either side of the road, in order to gain a view of the whole: *insulae* 7, 6, the street between 6 and 10, *insula* 10 (two-thirds of which is occupied by the House of Menander, I, 10, 4), and insula 8. Maiuri followed the Via dell'Abbondanza for 460 feet, to the point where it reached the amphitheater, which he also excavated, together with the *palaestra,* where the young men of Pompeii took their exercise. At the same time as he was completing work on the Villa of the Mysteries, he organized the digging of a trench over 26 feet wide around the whole of the outside of the city wall, which had been discovered by Murat as early as 1813–4. This was to allow him to study the structure of the walls and towers, and to restore Tower X.

Maiuri next turned his attention to the southern part of the city between the Via delle Scuole and the Triangular Forum, where the houses rise one behind the other up the slope of the hill. First, he determined to clear away all the volcanic debris that was stacked up against the hillside. And in this way, one of the most unusual features of Pompeii was restored: its characteristic appearance of a city constructed on many levels, with houses descending in terraces, commanding a spectacular view out over the steep drop and along the flank of the hill.

But Maiuri was not content to pursue his exploration of the buried city as a coherent whole. He felt it was only by deepening the excavations at the most significant, and topographically most important points—the forums, temples, city walls and oldest houses—that they could hope to shed light on the period of the city's origins, which were still obscure. For several years he carried out a systematic investigation of the pre-Roman and pre-Samnite strata. The discovery of the pre-Samnite city wall, in particular, allowed him to confirm the Greek influence that prevailed in the city after the battle of Cumae (474–450 B.C.). He pieced together the history of the Doric temple on the Triangular Forum in the Greek and Samnite periods; and he also proved that the Etruscan element of the population had participated in the life of the temple and the cult of Apollo during the period of Etruscan domination of Pompeii (525–474 B.C.). Excavations in the civil forum led to the discovery of a series of shops dating from the Paleo-Samnite era. These surrounded the open space of a square which covered the same surface area as the present forum, though it lay in a different direction and had no portico.

The remains of earlier dwellings found under private houses, such as the House of the Surgeon (VI, 1, 9, 10), led Maiuri to revise upward the date of the so-called limestone atrium ground-plan, to the middle and late Samnite periods, indicating clearly that the Pompeian atrium-house marks the end, rather than the beginning of a long sequence of development in municipal domestic design. Architectural surveys and analyses enabled Maiuri to pinpoint those elements of the city that date from its reconstruction after the earthquake of 62.

Credit must also go to Maiuri for much of the pleasure experienced by tourists in Pompeii, in that he was responsible for restoring the roofs of the

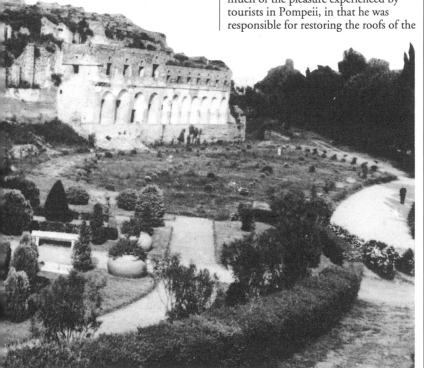

House of Menander (I, 10, 4), and the Villa of the Mysteries, without neglecting more modest dwellings such as the House of the Lovers (I, 7, 7) and the House of the Moralist (V, 1, 18). Nor did he neglect the restoration of public monuments, such as the tribunal of the basilica, the Tomb of the Istacidii, the row of columns around the Triangular Forum, as well as the exquisite monopteros around the sacred well there, built by the Samnite magistrate Numerius Trebius.

In September 1943 repeated bombardments added to the catalogue of disasters suffered by Pompeii since ancient times. Yet here, as elsewhere, the destruction often proved fruitful for archaeological science. Beneath the Antiquarium was found a villa that had not been robbed by the earthquake of its impressive paintings, and outside the city walls, in the suburb of S. Abbondio, the crater left by a bomb led to the discovery of the first blocks of a temple of Dionysos dating from the pre-Roman and Roman periods.

In 1951 work on the site was at last resumed, thanks to new resources… with the idea that the volcanic rubble cleared from Pompeii might be used to enrich the soil of the surrounding countryside. Of the 163 acres that make up the walled city, at least 64 acres had yet to be excavated, not including the areas just outside the walls and the suburbs. The first task was to excavate Regions I and II, which are separated by the *cardo* that leads out to the Nucerian Gate: *insulae* I, 9 and II, 3 were brought to light, and so too was II, 4, occupied entirely by the House of Julia Felix, which had previously been uncovered in 1755–7, only to be reburied! *Insula* 5 was found

to have been planted with a vineyard, and the Via dell'Abbondanza was followed to its end at the Sarnian Gate, a total of 3543 feet from the forum.

About 18 million cubic feet of earth and centuries-old debris were removed from around the city wall between the Marine Gate and the Greek theater, the Stabian Gate, and the amphitheater. And there now reappeared a view of the fine houses of Region VIII, whose large windows and terraces opened onto the panorama of the valley below, the mountains and the sea. The city wall was revealed to greater advantage, and above all the rich cemetery outside the Nucerian Gate provided a fresh harvest of inscriptions which shed light on the various classes of Pompeian society.

Over the last twenty years the excavations have continued under the guidance of A. de Franciscis, F. Zevi, and, most recently, Mrs. Irulli Cerulli: the House of Fabius Rufus has been uncovered in the *insula occidentalis*, to the west of Regions VI and VII, as well as that of C. Julius Polybius (IX, 13, 1–3). But worries as much as triumphs absorb the energies of the directors, as they attempt to conserve this highly prestigious site, which is visited by over a million people each year. Their main concern is to safeguard the Pompeian miracle, which, after many years of indifference, the Italian government has at last begun to treat with more sensitive awareness, since the intro-duction of special legislation in 1976.

Robert Etienne

Maiuri Through the Eyes of One of His Contemporaries

In his book Travels in Italy *the Italian writer Guido Piovene created a vivid portrait of the famous archaeologist.*

Maiuri in Pompeii, in raincoat and hat, 1955.

A little below average height, with one shoulder slightly lower than the other, Maiuri, this prince among archaeologists, seems to watch you out of the corner of his eye; obliquely, he envelops you in the gaze of his bright eyes, which, though they can sometimes be hard and piercing, are almost always gentle, with an extraordinary mobility of expression. It leaves you with the impression of having had as your guide the winged spirit which in Shakespeare's comedies leads the people lost in the forest. Maiuri walks with small steps, but he walks for hours at a stretch, as seems to be taught in the great school of archaeology. An archaeologist is not just an office worker, but a lover of the open air. And he has the knack —which, I am sad to say, seems to be dying out—of not imposing on you the great weight of his erudition, but only saying what he knows will be of interest to his interlocutor. In sum, he is one of the great lords of this lordly city, happy to welcome visitors to the site of the excavations and to do the honors.

Guido Piovene
Travels in Italy, 1958

The Cost of Living in Pompeii

The work of every archaeologist includes the collection of small indications and apparently insignificant objects that will allow the background to daily life to be meticulously reconstructed: for example, the prices for various goods in the currency of the period.

1 sesterce = 4 asses
1 denier = 4 sesterces

Foodstuffs

one *modius* (14 lbs.) of corn:	12 asses
one *modius* of wheat:	30 asses
one *modius* of lupins:	3 asses
one pound of oil:	4 asses
one measure of ordinary wine:	1 as
one measure of Falernian wine:	4 asses

Utensils

stewing pot:	1 as
plate:	1 as
small drinking vase:	2 asses
bucket:	9 asses
lamp:	1 as
silver sieve:	90 deniers

Clothing

tunic:	15 sesterces
for washing a tunic:	1 denier

Animals

mule:	520 sesterces

Slaves

two slaves: 5048 sesterces

The fact that the cost of living in Pompeii was relatively low is confirmed by the account book for a household of three people, including a slave, which reveals the contents of the Pompeian woman's "shopping basket" for the eight days before the Ides. The items are listed below:

8th day before the Ides

cheese:	1 as
bread:	8 asses
oil:	3 asses
wine:	3 asses
Total:	15 asses

7th day before the Ides

bread:	8 asses
oil:	5 asses
onions:	5 asses
stewing pot:	1 as
bread for slave:	2 asses
wine:	2 asses
Total:	23 asses

6th day before the Ides

bread:	8 asses
bread for slave:	4 asses
semolina:	3 asses
Total:	15 asses

5th day before the Ides

wine for the *domator* (trainer):	16 asses
bread:	8 asses
wine:	2 asses
cheese:	2 asses
Total:	28 asses

4th day before the Ides

hxeres (?):	16 asses
bread:	2 asses
femininum (?):	8 asses
hard wheat:	16 asses
bubella (?):	1 as
dates:	1 as
incense:	1 as
cheese:	2 asses
black pudding:	1 as
soft cheese:	4 asses
oil:	7 asses
Total:	59 asses

3rd day before the Ides

mountain *servato* (?):	17 asses
oil:	25 asses
bread:	4 asses
cheese:	4 asses
leek:	1 as
plate:	1 as
bucket:	9 asses
lamp:	1 as
Total:	62 asses

2nd day before the Ides

bread:	2 asses
bread for slave:	2 asses
Total:	4 asses

Day before the Ides

bread for slave:	2 asses
large loaf:	2 asses
leek:	1 as
Total:	5 asses

Ides

bread:	2 asses
large loaf:	2 asses
oil:	5 asses
semolina:	3 asses
for the *domator*, small fishes:	2 asses
Total:	14 asses

The Secret of the Villa of the Mysteries

The Villa of the Mysteries, a vast ninety-room mansion that was only discovered at the beginning of the 20th century, contains the most famous of all Pompeian frescoes. According to a recent study by Gilles Sauron, it seems that the cycle should be read not as a continuous frieze, but symmetrically along each wall, the frieze on the right representing the main stages in the apotheosis of Semele, and that on the left, the apotheosis of Dionysos.

Two separate but parallel series of images converge on the divine couple Dionysos and Semele (above left), guarantors of immortality. They illustrate the rites undergone by a lady of the Roman aristocracy as she is initiated into the Dionysiac cult.

The *domina* of the villa (below left), the priestess, is represented as a universal example. The most important moments of her life are placed in the context of successive episodes in the apotheosis of Semele and Dionysos.

The Myth of Semele

Semele's union with Zeus and the marriage of the priestess. The scene shows preparations for a wedding, in the presence of two Eros figures; one offers a mirror, while the other contemplates the scene, bow in hand.

Semele's pregnancy and the first initiation rite. A maenad turns toward a woman carrying a thyrsus, a staff entwined with vine leaves and ivy, which symbolizes the child that is about to be born.

The annihilation of Semele and the second initiation rite. From right to left: the initiate kneels to take refuge in the lap of a seated woman, whose hair is arranged in the traditional manner for wet-nurses and midwives. A winged demon is about to strike the initiate with a whip, symbolizing the lightning that killed Semele, while a torchbearer prepares to reveal the hidden phallus, a gesture that may represent childbirth. The scene as a whole symbolizes the priestess's participation in the annihilation of Semele, and therefore in her apotheosis.

The Myth of Dionysos

The education of Dionysos. A woman dressed in a peplos watches a young boy who is wearing nothing but a pair of high boots; he is reading, while a seated woman rests her right hand on his shoulder. In this image, the idea of study is related to that of initiation. The priestess is portrayed in her role as teacher, through both the figure of the secular mother and, in the context of the myth of Dionysos, that of the god's nurse.

The death of Dionysos and the priestess' role in the initiation of men into the Mysteries. Here, ritual actions are directly associated with the legend of the future god. A woman brings a plate piled with cakes; the priestess appears, crowned with an olive wreath, and lifts the corner of a veil that covers a basket. A servant pours a fine trickle of water onto the olive branch held out to her by her mistress. This no doubt refers to some funerary rite, the purpose of which is to prepare for the resurrection and apotheosis of Dionysos. The priestess is shown in her sacerdotal function, participating in the dramatic death of the god and in his implied resurrection.

The spreading of the Dionysiac cult and the priestess' initial fear before embracing the religion. Here we find the priestess, dressed as an elegant Greek citizen, in the center of a composition that includes the same three people, first on her right, and then on her left. She is terrified, as we can see from her expression and from the gesture of her left hand; the cloak billowing out above her head is a conventional way of indicating attempted flight. On her right, a Silenus figure crowned with a laurel wreath plays his lyre and sings a funeral dirge in honor of the dead Dionysos; two shepherds with goats' ears accompany him. On the left, the same three figures are preparing to present a spectacle, probably a dance.

The priestess is disturbed by the appearance of these representatives of an apparently barbarous and archaic religion. Yet while remembering the fears she experienced on the eve of her conversion, she shows that her misgivings were irrational and unfounded. For the god who finally appears at the center of the composition is the god of eternal youth, who, even on Mount Olympus, finds comfort in his mother's lap.

Universal and beneficent, Dionysos, far from encouraging ignorance among his rustic cortege of Silenus characters, urges the initiates to study books; literature is an essential stage on the route that leads to him.

The Boscoreale Treasure

In 1895 a man working on the excavation of a large villa at Boscoreale, not far from Pompeii, discovered at the bottom of a wine vat a horde of silver treasure, which a servant had no doubt hurriedly tried to protect at the time of the eruption. This complete set of Roman tableware can be seen today in the Louvre in Paris.

For a long time Roman society under the Republic refused, often with exaggerated scorn, to employ tableware made of precious metals; Pliny reports that the Carthaginian ambassadors received in Rome by senatorial families were astonished to find only two or three pieces from a single silver dinner service presented at every meal. The great treasures of the early Imperial period indicate the enormous changes brought about by the conquest of the East and the Carthaginian wars, which sent [gold] flooding into Rome.

Silver plate remained a luxury for a considerable time, however; a single

A mirror, with a bust of Dionysos. Above right, a silver cup with raised decoration illustrates the triumphal procession of Tiberius.

goblet often represented the only investment of a person of modest means, a soldier or shopkeeper, who would jealously have his name inscribed upon it. A collection as large as that from Boscoreale, made up of 109 pieces in all, could only have belonged to rich landowners, and even they would not have been able to purchase the service all in one go. Some particularly valuable pieces, considered essentially as works of art, may have been obtained as part of an inheritance—the three *phiales* with relief decoration, for example; but other objects passed from hand to hand, as we can see from the names of three successive owners inscribed on the base of the vases decorated with olive branches.

Although it remained the preserve of the rich, silver plate had nevertheless spread into every sphere of daily life by the early 1st century A.D., as we can judge from the fact that three elaborate mirrors, belonging to a lady's toilet, also formed part of the Boscoreale Treasure. The greater part of the collection is made up of items of tableware, drinking vessels, dishes, and other accessories.

Boscoreale does not perhaps offer the same range of forms as the treasure found in the House of Menander—a veritable typological repertoire of 1st-century Roman tableware—but it does provide examples of the most important items, many of which are grouped in pairs; the weight markings on the reverse of the objects often refer to the combined weight of the two matching pieces in a pair, rather than to that of the individual item.

Written and visual documents, particularly paintings and mosaics, often provide information on how the

various vessels were actually used. In spite of the richness of the decoration on some of the pieces, we should not forget that most of them would have been used, if not on a daily basis, then at least for important banquets; a fine array of silver tableware would have been the pride of every host. "Silverware, my very own silverware, is my great passion," proclaimed Trimalchio, Petronius' parvenu millionaire in the *Satyricon*.

Pergamum and Alexandria, the great centers of Hellenistic art, had attained a remarkably high standard of metalwork, and they had a direct influence on Rome, especially during the early years of the Empire. Not only objects, but also artists and artisans traveled from Greece to Italy, where they spread their techniques and repertoire of decorative motifs; the elaborate, yet elegant swirling foliage that decorates the lower portion of the wall around the *Ara Pacis* (Altar of Peace), erected in 13 B.C. to celebrate Augustus' return to Rome, was almost certainly inspired by Pergamanian silverware. Yet an almost identical pattern of plant stems curling symmetrically on either side of a vertical central stalk can be found on two of the drinking vases from Boscoreale; the composition is enlivened by the occasional animal appearing amid the leaves, or larger groups of creatures placed on large floral bouquets....

The same taste in decoration can be found in another context on two pairs of drinking vessels, one decorated with olive-tree leaves, the other with plane-tree branches; in the former, the rounded forms of the olives in high repoussé relief contrast with the smooth, flat surfaces and sharp angles of the leaves in lower relief, while in the latter, the curving silhouettes of the plane tree leaves are delicately outlined.

The motifs are not original, as goblets decorated with olives also formed part of the treasure from the House of Menander, but a comparison indicates the superior artistic and technical quality of those from Boscoreale; the fluidity of the lines and the careful rendering of details reveal the exceptional quality and high artistic value of this metalwork.

The same qualities—skill in execution, sensitivity to the decorative motif, and a taste for nature—can also be found in the crane and stork goblets, a highly suitable subject borrowed from Hellenistic art, and more specifically from Nile subjects, but treated here as a sequence of moments observed from life and presented rather in the manner of a comic strip. The "sufferings of a family of storks" show the parents struggling first with an undesirable host, then with a fellow scrounger, and finally with their starving offspring. Similarly, vases decorated with *xenia,* utensils, and food prepared for a banquet, depict an extremely appetizing succession of sketches: a trussed piglet, a hare, and a basket of fruits.

Petronius' vivid description of Trimalchio's feast provides us with abundant information about the richness and variety of the tableware that came to be used more and more widely, in the provincial cities as well as in Rome—a custom that even the Barbarians approved of.

In addition to plain containers, goblets, saucers, and trays, Petronius describes at great length the sumptuous tablecloths and precious vases decorated with mythological scenes. The highlight of the freedman's spectacle is the appearance on the table of a jointed silver skeleton, which offers him the opportunity of making a pompous speech about the brevity of life; here, farcical Epicurean maxims are placed in the mouth of a glutton, but this was also in fact the traditional theme of all Roman banquets, as the two famous skeleton goblets indicate.

Four tableaux on each vessel introduce the skeletons of Greek poets and philosophers—Sophocles, Menander, Zeno, and Epicurus, as well as other anonymous figures. The images are quite clear, but are supplemented by inscriptions, which point out who each one is, or draw out the moral of the scene; where one of the skeletons is weighing a heavy purse against a butterfly, symbol of the human soul, for example, the purse is labeled "wisdom." "Enjoy life while ye may," comments one inscription; "Life is a theater," states another. Black humor, quite common in Pompeii, can be either vicious—"Honor filth" is the sarcastic comment on the scene showing a skeleton offering a libation to his dead companion—or mocking:

A silver goblet (4.1 inches high), one of the most beautiful pieces in the Boscoreale Treasure. Skeletons are grouped in four separate scenes, beneath garlands of roses.

Epicurus seizes a huge portion of an enormous cake under the disapproving eye of Zeno. The Greek thinkers provide a warning presence in this interpretation of Epicurus' often-misunderstood philosophy.

Two goblets covered with Bacchic scenes bear witness to a completely different spirit. The origin of the motifs is the same, Hellenistic art, and these Dionysiac revels may remind us of the processions organized in Alexandria by Ptolemy VII, reviving memories of Bacchus' Indian triumph. Here, however, the motif appears in its most basic form, devoid of the religious significance that can be found, for instance, in certain paintings in Pompeii and, later, on sarcophagi. In this case it is the more picturesque and amusing aspects of the scene that have fired the silversmiths' imagination: the dainty putti, contrasted with the powerful lion and elephant —aspects of a Bacchic repertoire that frequently makes its appearance on drinking vessels in various guises, including masks, garlands, and more elaborate scenes.

The most impressive piece in the collection is without doubt the *phiale* decorated with an embossed head of Alexandria. It has been suggested that the young woman, who wears on her head the elephant skin that characterizes personifications of the Egyptian city, may be a portrait of Cleopatra VII. She is surrounded by a host of religious attributes evoking divinities of the Greco-Roman and Egyptian pantheons, an indication of the fervent experimentation with all forms of religion that occurred in certain parts of society toward the end of the Republic. This remarkably fine vessel, heightened by subtle gilding, is essentially a work of art which would probably have been displayed on a dresser for the admiration of guests, rather like the other two *phiales* in the Treasure, decorated with the repoussé portrait busts of an Augustan couple, and similar pieces in the Hildesheim Treasure.

Most of the objects from Boscoreale therefore derive their decoration from the familiar metalwork repertoire, and, in a more general way, from the minor Hellenistic arts. Certain motifs, however, adopted purely by Roman art, are direct borrowings from Greek prototypes: the Victories tearing the throats of their victims on a pair of *oenochoe,* for example, can be found in an identical form in Trajan's forum, and also on gold coins from Lampsacus (4th century B.C.).

Two exceptional items from the Treasure, held in a private collection, indicate the craftsmen's desire to employ this purely Roman repertoire. As early as the 3rd and 2nd centuries B.C., painters and sculptors were fond of depicting contemporary events in the native Italic tradition, and Roman art often shows that it had no qualms about juxtaposing elements from the Greek tradition with those evolved in a quite different context, in Rome itself. At the beginning of the 1st century B.C., for example, on the monument traditionally referred to as the Altar of Domitius Ahenobarbus, we find side by side a marine *thiasos* in the Scopas tradition and a historical relief, depicting scenes of census and sacrifice whose meaning is still in doubt. But what had until now been mere eclecticism, the arbitrary juxtaposition of two wholly different artistic

A silver cup (4 inches high) decorated with floral motifs and animals.

traditions, was molded under Augustus into a classical style, a perfect blend of the spirit of a past age with that of the present. The *Ara Pacis*, discussed earlier, is the most striking product of this fusion in the realm of official art; the Boscoreale is the finest example in the minor arts. Indeed, two goblets bear on their sides historical scenes which show, on the one hand, Augustus (receiving the *clipeus virtutis* awarded to the emperor by the Senate?) and, on the other, Tiberius.

The silver treasure from Boscoreale therefore offers a clear indication of the refinement of the Roman aristocracy and bourgeoisie at the beginning of the Imperial period; from this time on, the development of a clientele capable of

appreciating the products of the minor arts, combined with the move in taste toward increased luxury, resulted in a remarkable expansion in the production of such objects. The Boscoreale Treasure, which represents both a high level of technical achievement and growing confidence in decorative taste, in the choice of motifs and in their execution, through its combination of skill in the way the metal is worked and discreet application of gilding, bears witness both to the artistic ability of the metalworking ateliers and to the luxurious living conditions of the wealthy Campanian landowners.

François Baratte
Archeologia, no. 54, January 1973

The Second Death of Pompeii

What Vesuvius spared in 79, humans are now in the process of destroying. The Italian government has blocked the 36 million lire earmarked by the European Community in 1984 for the restoration of Pompeii. Vegetation, humidity, vandalism, and hordes of tourists are finishing off the ghost town. It is an archaeological tragedy of the first order.

Pompeii, Easter 1979: there is a vast crowd of tourists. Among the buildings stands a private house not open to the public, where, in the atrium, or inner courtyard, the stone columns are still standing. It is impossible to keep an eye on everyone. Some of the tourists find their way into the courtyard and, as a game, start to push against the columns. Eventually they succeed in knocking them down. "Fun" like this is apparently quite common. Indeed, it is reported that there are even competitions to see who can bring the columns down quickest. Give or take a month, it was then 1900 years since Vesuvius' destruction of the city. The two events are not without their parallels.

Archaeologists who know Pompeii well have a great deal to say on the subject. For even since 1980, when an earthquake caused much damage to the famous site, Pompeii has been the scene of a permanent catastrophe. Year by year, day by day, the city is being destroyed—and largely by people.

It must be used to it by now. Seventeen years before the disaster that buried it, the city was devastated by an earthquake. At the time of the eruption several buildings had just been rebuilt, while others were still being restored. The wool market, for example, had lost part of its rubble facade; this section had been replaced with brick, but the facing had yet to be applied to disguise the discordant mixture of materials—when suddenly, 24 August 79 dawned.

But just when Pompeii was being "revived," according to the accepted phrase, it began to die its second death. Not only because the early excavations, carried out over two hundred years ago and again in the 19th century, often turned out to be more of a massacre—what fun to carry off statues and fling around inscribed bronze plaques!—but also because all the remains preserved by the catastrophic eruption, were now exposed to the extremes of the weather, to vegetation, and to human beings.

Even before the most recent earthquake, the situation was not ideal. But Pompeii nevertheless retained its attractive appearance; photographers could still enjoy working there. The shocks of 23 November 1980 sent columns, whole walls or sections of wall, and certain upper stories crashing to the ground, and left several others leaning dangerously. Entire areas of the city were closed to visitors; props and struts were introduced. As elsewhere in Italy, the entrance fee was suddenly increased: from 150 to 4000 lire.

In 1983 the authorities in charge of the site asked the French archaeologist Jean-Pierre Adam to prepare a technical report on the damage sustained by the city, to evaluate all possible methods of restoration and the various remedies that could be employed. In 1984 the European Community awarded the sum of 36 million lire for the restoration of Pompeii, the first payment to be made available from the beginning of 1985.

Was Pompeii about to be rescued? In 1985 a new superintendent was appointed. He promised to implement all the report's findings. Yet the result was a complete stoppage to all archaeological work on the site. Of course, archaeologists continued to travel from all over the world to see what was going on, in their own time and paying their own expenses. They returned dismayed. In spite of the efforts of their Italian colleagues, in spite of the huge increase in entrance tariffs and the considerable size of the available budget, in spite of the drastic reduction of the area open to the public, the situation was not improving; in fact, if anything, it was getting worse. The report has still not produced any results. No work has been commissioned, no contract has been signed with the excellent institutes of restoration that exist within Italy itself, in Florence and in Rome, and which are generally considered the best in the world. The 36 billion lire are waiting, they say, for "technical and administrative problems which have yet to be resolved."

Some damage is caused quite innocently. The site receives about half a million visitors a year; it has become the great public park of the Naples region, filled with buildings, and it welcomes an average 4500 tourists on each opening day. Almost 22,000 visitors have been counted on certain Easter Mondays. These visitors, inevitably, walk around, and in walking they wear down the roads. In particular, they wear down any pavements left in antiquity without a stone covering. Below the surface of these pavements run lead drains, ancient drains reconstructed after the earthquake of 62, and placed at that time—provisionally, so they thought— not far from the surface. Little by little the tourists erode the soil, until these lead pipes are uncovered; they tread on them; the lead is crushed, cracks, and eventually often disappears altogether.

The stone-covered sidewalk suffers, too. Cracks open up in the mortar or in the mosaic of pebbles. Bit by bit, the covering, trampled and kicked, falls to pieces. Only the paving slabs of the streets themselves stand up to this harsh treatment, as these were always carved from solid lava and were designed to withstand the passage of the carts. The edges of the sidewalk, however, are often made of volcanic tufa or limestone, soft stones that are eroded by the constant wear and tear, worn down, and deformed. This happened in Roman times, too, but then they would have been replaced. Visitors to Pompeii should surely be made to walk in the street, not on the sidewalk. In the famous Via dell'Abbondanza the constant passage of feet has worn the

sidewalk down to the same level as the road, and in some places even below it.

Graffiti continue to multiply, the vandals preferring to leave their mark on the few paintings that are still in good condition. People pull gently at the edge of a layer of plaster that is starting to come away—and there are plenty of these. They get into the forbidden areas, by clambering over the barriers or by whatever other means they can find, and amuse themselves to the extent of committing acts of vandalism, pure and simple....

Another favorite pastime is to pick up remains, to carry off small pieces of stucco or pottery, or fragments of marble. Paintings are particularly popular. Not to be carried away in one piece to be offered for sale later—that would be too difficult. Instead, the best part—a decorative motif, a human figure, an animal, a small tableau—is roughly hacked out. This kind of activity is not a recent development, of course; it represents the continuation of an age-old practice. Traditions die hard in Campania, whether they are encouraged by tourists or faithfully maintained by the inhabitants of the region.

In reading books on Pompeii, people are often surprised by the small number of minor objects found there—statuettes, for example—even on the site of recent excavations. This rarity is even more striking because the houses excavated in Herculaneum by American archaeologists retained, by contrast, all their smaller objects. And yet the two cities were both victims of the same eruption. Many other countries have experienced what could be called "bargain-offer" excavations. But in Pompeii, this exceptional site, the disappearance of objects seems to have reached a worrying level. There is practically nothing left that could be carried away in a pocket or a bag. The authorities have even had to give up leaving copies of antique objects (casts and false bronzes), let alone any original furniture in place, which would have constituted an exceptional history lesson for visitors.

"Obviously," says Jean-Pierre Adam, "the archaeologists and authorities do not know what is happening, and even if they did, there is precious little they could do about it. You must remember that we are not far from Naples. Furthermore, the managers of the site are virtually obliged to employ local firms to carry out restoration work on Pompeii. These firms, who may be quite well versed in current building techniques, are completely incompetent when it comes to matters of restoration." Restoration work requires scrupulous care and extensive knowledge of specialized techniques. These conditions are not always met. And so,

paradoxically, we see the restoration work hastening the deterioration it was intended to prevent.

Sometimes it is the fault of ancient work; they did not know any better. Perhaps they were not aware that lintels over window and door openings should be replaced with hard wood suitably seasoned to prevent rot and mold. Soft wood, insufficiently treated, quickly succumbs to attack; wood-eating insects move in, with disastrous consequences. Some mistakes are notorious: in the House of Meleager, in the northwest of the city, the roof timbers for a room 16 by 36 feet, designed to support the weight of over 5 tons of tiles, were erected with no triangular sections to give it strength; in spite of attempts to reinforce the roof with steel, the structure collapsed.

Sadly, the reinforced concrete used on the site was often, according to the report's findings, "particularly badly mixed." Was this the result of repeated mistakes or of small savings on the cost of the materials? The concrete flakes away; the steel skeleton, exposed to the air, begins to rust and to expand, hastening the destruction of the building. Similar faults can be found in many of the mortar coatings applied to protect areas of ancient masonry. The poor-quality mortar, which contains too much sand, tends to crack as it ages; soon water and vegetation start to penetrate.

This same uncertain mixture of incompetence and roguery can be seen in the restoration of painted plaster wall surfaces. The workmen of ancient times used iron ties to attach the surface layers to the masonry behind them, but not only are these ugly, they also rust, expanding and cracking the plaster all around them. Yet more modern alternatives are scarcely any better.

To reattach the plaster to the masonry without having to remove it completely, they start by removing the crumbling edges from the surface that is to be consolidated. They then remove the old mortar using an iron rod poked up from below between the facing and its support. The gap is refilled with a liquid concrete poured down into the gap from above. Problems arise from the fact that the removal of the old mortar can never be complete. If it were, the whole surface would disintegrate, in spite of the supporting struts. So they leave some in place, which means that after the pouring process, there are two different types of mortar next to each other; being of a different composition, they react in different ways, causing cracks to form. This has resulted in the collapse of whole areas of wall surface.

The new mortar does not even fill the entire space. Investigations were carried out on a painted wall in the House of the Pygmies, restored in 1979; the height of the area being treated was 4.5 feet, but the new liquid mortar ran down at best only 9 inches, and at worst, a mere 1.5 inches. The flows of plaster were not even contiguous. In addition, the load-bearing masonry was not treated at all, so after a short time they had to repeat the process all over again. Once more, they had to scratch away at the edges of the top layer of plaster, and so on, until the whole thing had disappeared.

Clearly, the work of the 1st-century builders of Pompeii does not always help the 20th-century restorers. Analyses carried out in Paris show that, even where the plaster surfaces were executed with great care, what lay behind them was not necessarily of the same quality. The lime content of the mortar was often rather low, and this antique mortar, originally designed to save money, crumbles easily. It can even be eroded by the wind. In damp areas, it encourages rising damp, which damages the painted murals. It is the difference in lime content between the wall and its covering that causes so many plaster surfaces to become detached. And finally, in the rubble of the wall itself, a variety of different materials was often used.

Farmers have always prized the land around Mount Vesuvius, because the soil there is some of the most fertile in the world. Several feet thick, the topsoil abounds in rapidly absorbed mineral salts, thanks to Vesuvius. In the time of Augustus, at the beginning of the 1st century A.D., the geographer Strabo wrote that, in certain parts of Campania, you could get two wheat harvests, a third of millet, and sometimes even a fourth of vegetables. Even today, farmers in the region grow several crops of early vegetables, even planting them in the orchards. The same rich soil, only in a thinner layer, lies beneath Pompeii. The result is catastrophic.

Thirty-one parasitic plant varieties have been identified on the site by G. Aymonin of the National Museum for Natural History. There is a whole collection of weeds, from acanthus to wild carrot, from the fiercesome fennel and dreadful fig, to bindweed and brambles. First, the plants invade patches of bare earth. In the areas visited by tourists, the battle against the weeds is relatively easy, as the visitors' feet now become our allies. But in the houses that are closed to the public, enclosed areas of bare soil—in the peristyles, gardens, atria—are rapidly covered with a dense mat of vegetation, which soon reaches out toward the surrounding walls and attacks them. This is a particular problem in the most badly ruined houses close to the sectors that have not yet been excavated.

Vegetation also attacks concrete floors and their decoration. It can utterly destroy mosaic floors. As soon as a single one of the tiny cubes disappears, a plant will come and take root there. It

is even possible for the roots of plants outside to force off the revetments. Most visitors are blissfully unaware of all this. They see no more than five or six houses, all of which are well kept, and remain quite oblivious of what is quietly being destroyed elsewhere. For the traveling exhibition on Pompeii that toured Europe recently, a plan was drawn up showing the areas of flooring in the excavated portion of the city that still have their original stone or marble coverings. They now constitute only a very small percentage of the total surface area. Yet when they were first excavated, they were all covered, every single one—with mortar in the case of the more humble dwellings, and with mosaics in the case of the richest. Thousands of square feet of floor covering must have disintegrated and simply ceased to exist. And the destruction continues.

Stonework may also be destroyed, when the covering has disappeared and the facing has been damaged or fallen away. On the tops of walls, brambles, fennel, and broom take hold, soon forming a great mass of vegetation that results in falling masonry. Along the inside walls, valerian and brambles cling to the surfaces and dig their roots into the stonework, working their way under the facings. The roots grow, thicken, burying themselves ever more deeply. Cracks open up, also allowing damp to enter. Ivy, too, plays its part; it clings to the facings and weighs on them, encouraging them to come away. It is attached to the facing more tightly than the facing is attached to the wall, so when people try to remove the ivy, the whole surface of the wall comes away with it.

Of course, all it would take is a small army of careful and dedicated cleaners to take up arms against these plagues. Plus a team of expert restorers.... Today, in the parts of Pompeii that are still closed to the public, you will find walls buried under a mass of vegetation, fissured masonry, cracked columns, and crumbling mosaics in which one piece after another is falling away; invading plants, combined with damp, human damage and neglect, are threatening the site as much as the instability of the ground upon which it stands. There are houses which have been excavated, but which you can no longer enter because of the weeds growing there. Close to the unexcavated areas, some courtyards of the ancient houses have been transformed into jungles, which, left to their own devices, attack, crack, and destroy at will.

It is a slow, gradual tragedy that will leave not a wrack behind. Pompeii has become the sorry example of how not to proceed in matters of restoration. It is a major archaeological disaster.

Henri de Saint-Blanquat
Science et Avenir, no. 469
March 1986

An Archaeological Itinerary

Although Pompeii is one of the best archaeological sites in the world, any visitor to the region should not miss the many important sites nearby, especially those shown here.

With its patrician villas looking out over the sea, its public monuments, and its mild climate, Herculaneum rivaled the neighboring city of Pompeii.

Stabiae, with its villas and baths, lay a few miles south of Pompeii; it was buried by the lava that flowed from Vesuvius in August 79.

Naples.
Herculanum
Oplontis
Boscoreale
Pompei
Stabies

GOLFO

NAPOLI

Oplontiš, which experts agree was on the site of present-day Torre Annunziata, has provided us with one of the finest suburban houses, the villa of Sabina Poppaea.

In antiquity Boscoreale, on the slopes of Vesuvius above Pompeii, was made up of several farming estates and their villas; in one, a horde of silver treasure was discovered.

Glossary

aedile Town magistrate: two elected annually to supervise the day-to-day administration of the city

ala (pl. **alae**) Side wing, opening to right or left at the far end of an atrium

amphora Two-handled vessel for liquids, especially wine, usually made of clay

apochae Receipts issued by a creditor, acknowledging payment of debt

apodyterium Changing or undressing room at the baths

atlantes Supports in the form of carved male figures

augustales Group of freedmen who celebrated the cult of the emperor, instituted by Tiberius in honor of Augustus

basilica Colonnaded public hall on the forum, used for commercial transactions and the dispensing of justice

caldarium Hot room in the baths

carcer (pl. **carceres**) Underground room at the amphitheater where gladiators and wild beasts waited their turn

cardo Road from north to south

cavea (**ima**, **media**, **summa**) Lower, middle and top sections of tiered seating in the theater or amphitheater

cella Main body of a classical temple, housing the cult statue

comitium Meeting place on the forum where magistrates assembled for voting

compluvium Square central opening in the roof over the domestic atrium

curia Senate house on the forum, where the decurion council met

decumanus Road from east to west

decurio (pl. **decuriones**) Members of the council, often former magistrates

dolium (pl. **dolia**) Large earthenware jar, globular in form, with a wide mouth

duovir (pl. **duoviri**) Two senior magistrates of a colony, elected annually by the whole plebiscite, who presided over the decurion council and had law-giving powers

frigidarium Cold room at the baths

fullonica Fulling works or tannery

garum Fish sauce

Herm Name derived from early Greek statues of Hermes in the form of a rectangular shaft with a carved head. Later, they could carry the heads of other divinities

horti pompeiani Suburban market gardens of Pompeii

impluvium Pool in the center of an atrium, immediately below the *compluvium* (see above)

insula Block of townhouses

lararium Household shrine dedicated to the *lares*

lares Tutelary deities, originally from Etruscan religion, worshiped as the protectors of a particular locality. Most common are the *lares familiares* or *domestici*, the household gods; *lares compitales* are the gods of the crossroads

lictor (pl. **lictores**) Freeborn attendant granted to a magistrate as a sign of official dignity

ludus (pl. **ludi**) Public games or spectacles

macellum Market

magister (pl. **magistri**) Magistrates; *magistri vici et compiti* magistrates of the quarter and of the crossroads

monopteros Temple consisting of a single row of columns supporting a roof

oecus Richly decorated salon or drawing room

palaestra Sports ground, from the Greek for a wrestling school

patera Broad, flat dish or saucer used especially for offerings

peristyle Inner courtyard surrounded by a colonnade, of Hellenistic inspiration

podium Raised base of a temple, or parapet wall around the first row of seats at the amphitheater

Priapus Rustic god of fertility, often portrayed with a huge penis

res publica Public service

retiarius Type of gladiator, net-fighter

sistrum Metallic rattle used in religious ceremonies

strigil Scraper made of horn or metal used by bathers to remove impurities from the skin

tablinum Central room at the far end of the atrium, often used as the main reception room

tabulae ceratae Wax-covered wooden tablets used for writing

tepidarium Warm room in the baths

thermopolium Tavern or bar serving warm drinks

tholos Beehive-shaped chamber built of stone

thyrsus Long staff entwined with ivy and vine leaves, and often tipped with a pine cone, carried by Dionysos and his followers

triclinium Dining room in a Roman house or in the open air

uraeus Egyptian cobra sacred to Isis

velum Canopy suspended over the seats at a theater or amphitheater

venatio Hunting or the combat of wild beasts

vicini Inhabitants of a quarter, neighbors

vicomagister Freedman responsible for the cult of the *lares compitales* (see *lares* and *magister* above), from *vicus*, quarter

Further Reading

Andrews, Ian, *Pompeii*, Cambridge University Press, New York, 1978

d'Arms, John H., *Romans on the Bay of Naples*, Harvard University Press, Cambridge, 1970

Biel, Timothy L., *Pompeii*, Lucent Books, San Diego, 1989

Boethius, Axel, *Etruscan and Early Roman Architecture*, Penguin Books, New York, 1970

Boissier, Gaston, *Rome and Pompeii: Archaeological Rambles*, trans. by D. Havelock Fisher, repr. of 1896 ed., Irvington, New York

Bradway, Katherine, *Villa of Mysteries: Pompeii Initiation Rites of Women*, C. G. Jung, San Francisco

Brion, Marcel, *Pompeii and Herculaneum: The Glory and the Grief*, Crown Publications, New York, 1960

Corti, Egon C., *The Destruction and Resurrection of Pompeii and Herculaneum*, trans. by K. and R. Gregor Smith, Routledge and Kegan Paul, London, 1951

Curtis, Robert I., ed., *Studia Pompeiana et Classica in Honor of Wilhelmina F. Jashemski, Vol. I: Pompeiana*, Caratzas, New Rochelle, New York, 1989

Deiss, Joseph J., *Herculaneum, Italy's Buried Treasure*, Harper and Row, New York, 1985

Franklin, James L., *Pompeii: The Electoral Programmata, Campaigns and Politics 71–79*, Pennsylvania State University Press, University Park, Pennsylvania, 1980

Goor, Ron and Nancy, *Pompeii: Exploring a Roman Ghost Town*, Harper and Row Junior Books, New York, 1986

Grant, Michael, *Cities of Vesuvius: Pompeii and Herculaneum*, Penguin Books, New York, 1971

———, *Eros in Pompeii: The Secret Rooms of the National Museum of Naples*, Morrow, New York, 1975

Humphrey, Kathryn L., *Pompeii: Nightmare at Midday*, Watts, New York, 1990

Jashemski, Wilhelmina F., *The Gardens of Pompeii, Herculaneum and the Villas Destroyed by Vesuvius*, Caratzas, New Rochelle, New York, 1979

Jongman, William, *The Economy and Society of Pompeii*, Benjamins North America, Philadelphia, 1988

Kraus, Theodor, and Leonard von Matt, *Pompeii and Herculaneum: the Living Cities of the Dead*, trans. by Robert G. Wolf, Harry N. Abrams, New York, 1975

Kunhardt, Edith, *Pompeii…Buried Alive!*, Random House, New York, 1987

Leppmann, Wolfgang, *Pompeji: Eine Stadt in Literatur und Leben*, Nymphenburger, München, 1966

Little, Alan, *Roman Bridal Drama*, Moretus Press, Ossining, New York, 1978

Lloyd, Alan, *The Taras Report on the Last Days of Pompeii*, International Specialized Book Services, Portland, Oregon, 1977

Mau, August, *Pompeii: Its Life and Art*, trans. by Francis W. Kelsey, Caratzas, New Rochelle, New York, 1982

McKay, Alexander G., *Houses, Villas, and Palaces in the Roman World*, Cornell University Press, Ithaca, New York, 1975

Richardson, L., Jr., *Pompeii: An Architectural History*, Johns Hopkins, Baltimore, Maryland, 1988

Rosen, Mike, *The Destruction of Pompeii*, Watts, New York, 1988

Salmon, Edward T., *The Making of Roman Italy*, Cornell University Press, Ithaca, New York, 1982

———, *A History of the Roman World from 30 B.C. to A.D. 138*, Methuen, London, 1968

Trevelyan, Raleigh, *The Shadow of Vesuvius: Pompeii A.D. 79*, Joseph, London, 1976

List of Illustrations

Index

Acknowledgments

We wish to thank the following: Mrs. Bonaiutti of the Centre Jean-Bérard, Naples; Claude Albore-Livadie, researcher, CNRS, Naples; The Pagliara Foundation, University Institute Suor Orsola Benincasa, Naples; Jean-Pierre Adam, Dept of Classical Architecture, Vincennes; Gilles Sauron of the University of Dijon; Mrs. Samson, head of photographic services, Bibliothèque Nationale, Paris; Claude Moatti, historian; Editions Grasset; the reviews *Archeologia* and *Science et Avenir*. Seneca, *Naturales Questiones*, vols. VII and X, trans. by T. H. Corcoran, Harvard University Press, Cambridge, Mass., 1971, reprinted by permission of the publishers and The Loeb Classical Library; *Letters of the Younger Pliny*, trans. © B. Radice, 1963 (Penguin Classics, 1969), reproduced by permission of Penguin Books Ltd; Goethe, *Italian Journey*, trans. W. H. Auden and E. Mayer, © 1962 Pantheon Books, reprinted by permission of HarperCollins and Curtis Brown, Ltd; Stendhal, *Rome, Naples and Florence*, trans. Richard N. Coe, © John Calder (Publishers) Ltd, 1959, reprinted by permission of the Calder Educational Trust, London. Map and line drawings: Patrick Mérienne 46–7, 186.

Photograph Credits

Jean-Pierre Adam, Paris 198–203, 205. Archiv für Kunst und Geschichte, Berlin 19*b*, 28–9, 48, 51, 61, 163, 170, 173. Artephot/Held, Paris 72*r*, 115. Artephot/Mandel, Paris 116. Artephot/Nimatallah, Paris 83, 126, 129. Artephot/Percheron, Paris 64*c*. Artephot/Ziolo, Paris 128*a*. Didier Baussy, Paris 17*a* and *b*, 49*b*, 59*b*, 142. Bibliothèque de l'Institut, Paris 147. Bibliothèque Nationale, Paris 19*a*, 22*a* and *b*, 24, 25, 26–7, 52–3*a*, 65, 86–7, 88*b*, 99*a* and *b*, 103*a* and *b*, 107*a*, 110–1, 117, 135, 136, 143, 146, 149, 150–1. M.E. Boucher, Boulogne 43, 49*c*, 59*a*. Bulloz, Paris 55*a*, 56–7*a*, 82. Chuzeville, Paris 93, 107*b*, 111*b*, 192–7. Dagli-Orti, Paris 69*b*, 77, 78*b*, 91*a* and *b*, 102, 112, 131. Dieuzaide, Toulouse 12–3. Edimédia, Paris 141. ENSBA, Paris 32–3, page preceding gatefold, gatefold following 32 1 and 2, 35, 36–7*a* and *b*, 42, 74*b*, 97*b*, gatefold following 104, page following gatefold, 104–5. Explorer/Krafft, Paris 11. Giraudon, Paris 14–5, 66, 113. Hubert Josse, Paris 10. Magnum/Lessing, Paris 49*a*, 69*a*, 97, 98, 118*a*, 124. Musée de l'Assistance Publique, Paris 144. Nasjonalgalleriet, Oslo 45. National Trust, London 20–1. Rapho, Paris 202*b*. Rapho/Lawson 125. Rapho/Tholy 97. Rapho/Von Matt 64*b*, 185. RMN, Paris 100–1. Rights reserved 44, 79, 106*a*, 128*b*, 130*br*, 138, 139*b*, 152, 159, 167, 202*a*. Robert Etienne, Bordeaux 74–5*a*, 74*b*, 80, 81*a* and *b*, 88*a*, 94. Roger-Viollet, Paris 30*a* and *b*, 31, 39, 40, 56–7*b*, 60*a*, 63, 70, 71*a*, 72*l*, 73, 76, 78*a*, 94*b*, 118*b*, 119, 134, 139*a*, 140, 153–4, 157, 158, 160, 161, 166, 178, 179, 180. Rotondo, Naples 18, 24, 41, 148, 155, 182. Jean Roubier, Paris 60*c*. Scala, Florence 54, 67, 84–5, 90, 92, 114, 120–3, 127, 130*a*, 186–91. Société de Géographie, Paris 168–9. Victoria and Albert Museum, London 132–3. U.D.F., Paris 55*b*, 62, 89, 108–9. Werner Forman Archives, London 68.

Robert Etienne discovered the enduring fascination of Pompeii in 1939, when he read F. Thédenat's study of the city. He first visited Pompeii and studied its wealth of archaeological material in 1948, while he was a member of the Ecole de Rome. In 1951 he was commissioned to prepare a book on daily life in Pompeii, and he twice stayed there during the month of August, in order to relive the anniversary of the catastrophe on the very spot where it had occurred. For the past twenty-five years he has regularly returned to Pompeii for periods of study, and he shares the concern of all those who are alarmed by the gradual decay of this famous ancient city. Today Robert Etienne is professor at the University of Bordeaux.

For Emmanuelle and Véronique

Translated from the French by Caroline Palmer

Project Manager: Sharon AvRutick
Typographic Designer: Elissa Ichiyasu
Design Assistant: Tricia McGillis
Editorial Assistant: Jennifer Stockman

Library of Congress Catalog Card Number: 91–75506

ISBN 0–8109–2855–8

Copyright © Gallimard 1987

English translation copyright © 1992 Harry N. Abrams, Inc., New York, and Thames and Hudson Ltd., London

Published in 1992 by Harry N. Abrams, Incorporated, New York
A Times Mirror Company

Printed and bound in Italy by Editoriale Libraria, Trieste